A Matter of Principle

James Starke

ISBN: 978-1-7343083-7-2 Library of Congress Control Number: 2020942052

Front cover image is a drawing by Donna Kato.
Original book design by JetLaunch.
First printing edition 2020. This printing: 2022.

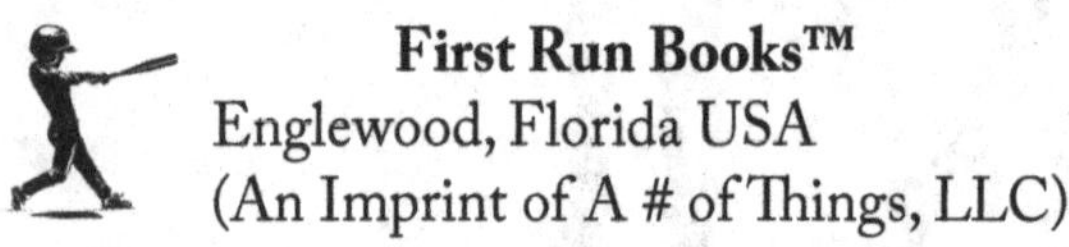

First Run Books™
Englewood, Florida USA
(An Imprint of A # of Things, LLC)

Dedication

To Brittany, who always wanted
to be a lawyer someday.

Forward

You may have noticed from the copyright page that this book was written in 1991.

This is more than 3 decades before the tumultuous summer of 2022, when the U.S. Supreme Court revealed itself as the reactionary institution many observers had accused it of becoming, the end result of a concerted effort over many years to ensconce conservative ideology into the high court.

There is a belief by some people that decisions of the Supreme Court have always been political. That is somewhat true in the past but surely it has been nothing like this. In the 2020s the Court came out of the closet, becoming more overtly political, the justices protestations to the contrary notwithstanding.

The legal reasoning offered by them in support of their decisions read more like rationalizations to reach a desired result consistent with their political beliefs than any fair, balanced and consistent interpretation of the Constitution. These days the only consistent way to predict a ruling in any given case is to consult the individual political beliefs of the justices and then do a head count.

And so it has come to pass that, in both practice and perception, the Supreme Court has devolved from being an ostensibly apolitical institution into one that gleefully embraces one of two extremes in a bi-polar political spectrum gripping America in the 2020s.

The Court of the 1980s seems tame by comparison.

Back then, the world was not that far removed from the protest era of the 1960s and 70s. To be sure, America had turned away from the idealism of those earlier times, becoming more cynical as a way to better rationalize the pursuit of material things to the exclusion of pretty much everything else.

Yet, yuppie though they were, American youth in the 80s liked the idea that out there, somewhere, there were still a few idealists who were fighting the good fight, making the world more free, maybe not so much for speeding motorists but for the many causes they secretly held dear.

Four centuries ago, *The Ingenious Gentleman Don Quixote of La Mancha* may have similarly intrigued the people of Spain. In what was the first – and some say the best – literary work of all time, Miguel de Cervantes had introduced a character who had an idealistic view of the world.

While quirky and at times seemingly insane, at least Don Quixote offered *something* more than the banal, hedonistic pursuit of material things that defines the existence of so many people.

There is a reason that *Don Quixote* is so well regarded centuries after it was first published.

Most thoughtful people want to believe that there is something more to life than this vale of tears.

At least they used to.

They want to believe that there are people out there who are still willing to charge forward on their trusty steeds, lance in hand, loyal sidekick at their side, fighting the good fight, championing the cause of chivalry, honor, justice, and the betterment of all humankind.

But, for the time being at least, woe be to the knight that tilts in the direction of the Supreme Court.

www.amatterofprinciple.info

CONTENTS

CHAPTER I
THE INITIATION

One day, Earl decided to see how fast his car could go. He heard from somewhere that pushing a car to its top speed blew away a bunch of carbon that had built up in its carburetor, making the engine run more smoothly. Anyway, that was the theory, or excuse, as the case may be.

After making this bold decision, Earl braced himself and gently pushed the accelerator to the floor of his 454 Monte Carlo. He was not a particularly wild and impetuous young man. In fact, his friends in high school always told him he had a "Boy Scout" mentality. He had to loosen up, they said. So now he found himself trying to do something completely foolish, like a young man who just finished high school is supposed to do.

The car lurched forward as the four-barrel kicked massive doses of flammable liquid into the bowels of the churning engine, propelling Earl and half a ton of steel forward at a perilous rate of speed. As the needle on the speedometer crept past the 100-mile-per-hour mark, Earl glanced sideways and noticed the trees and other vegetation on the side of the highway were whizzing by at a dizzying pace. When he looked again at the speedometer, he saw that he had reached the 125-mile-per-hour mark.

The car began to shake.

Deciding that surely by now any carbon was probably gone, he eased the car back down to a rational speed. As the car slowed and the trees became less of a blur, a light rain started to fall. Earl noticed for the first time that all of his muscles were tense and locked into place. He allowed his body to go slack and the breath he had been holding to leave his lungs.

Then a glimmer of blue light from the rearview mirror caught the corner of his eye.

A sickening feeling began to rise from the pit of Earl's stomach at the first sight of the telltale blue light. Like many motorists caught red-handed, for a brief moment he entertained the silly thought that the officer was after someone else, that by just slowing down and making promises heavenward, the police cruiser would scream past, leaving him to breathe a sigh of relief.

Never again, he thought to himself, *if I can just be spared this one time*. But in his heart of hearts, Earl knew for whom the blue lights flashed.

They flashed for him.

The Florida Highway Patrol Trooper stubbornly refused to go around Earl, even after he had slowed down to farm tractor speed. With a heavy sigh and a curse, Earl finally pulled his race car onto the shoulder of Interstate Highway 75. He moaned to himself, watching from his side mirror as the trooper advanced to the driver's side of the car. He had already pulled together his license and registration, handing them out the window to the trooper when he arrived.

"Mind stepping out of the car, sir?"

He must think I am some sort of desperado on a high-speed chase or something, Earl thought to himself. "Is there something wrong, Officer?" he asked as he stepped out of the car.

"Yeah, you were speeding," replied the trooper.

The light rain was turning into a steady drizzle, so the trooper invited Earl back to his cruiser while he finished filling out his paperwork. Earl made a point of being polite and respectful. But the die had been cast, and he knew it.

"You know, this is the most dangerous time, when the rain first starts to fall," said the trooper in a kindly tone, motioning towards the highway and the inhospitable rain that began to fall with greater authority, pounding on the roof of the cruiser.

"I wasn't aware of that, sir."

"When the water first hits the pavement, the oils gather at the surface, creating sort of an oil slick that can make a vehicle skid out of control. Later, as the rain continues, it washes away the oils and the road becomes a little bit safer."

"I didn't know that."

"I'm concerned about your safety, son. That's the point of all this, you know." The trooper turned to look at Earl, giving him an earnest expression.

"I realize that, Officer."

"I don't suppose there was some sorta dire emergency that made you go so fast?"

"No, sir." Earl was on his way up to visit his older brother at the university he himself was to attend later that year. He didn't think the urgency of getting to a college campus for a keg party qualified as a bona fide emergency.

"Do you realize how fast you were going?"

"No, sir."

The trooper motioned towards the flashing red digital readout of the number "98" on the radar equipment attached to the dashboard. The red "98" continued to flash accusatorily while the trooper continued with his paperwork.

After he received his citation and was sent on his merry way, Earl was careful not to exceed the speed limit by more than five miles per hour. There was an unwritten rule he heard about from somewhere that you could go a little bit over the limit so long as you didn't abuse the privilege. The longer-than-usual ride gave him more time to think about a lot of things, in addition to his bouts of paranoia when he saw a car along the side of the road or one in the distance that seemed like it had a rack of lights on the roof that disappeared like a mirage when he got closer.

Earl imaged himself to be an old man trapped in the body of a teenager. He was not prone to such flights of fancy or acting on impulse. This speeding thing was an aberration, although on occasion he did find his body doing things that his mind could scarcely believe. There was a person deep down inside of him that every once in a while came to the surface and took control when his mature, rational self was caught unawares. During the times that this crazy person came out of hiding, Earl usually found himself in some sort of trouble.

This speeding ticket deal was a case in point.

The real Earl – the one who had graduated early from high school, was working two jobs to save money for school, and was accepted to the big university because he scored so well on his SAT – had carefully plotted a course for his future. He had researched the facts and planned exactly how he would make his way into his chosen profession: the law.

There was no doubt in his mind that he had the soul of a lawyer. Mr. and Mrs. Warren had not particularly encouraged their son to become a lawyer. They were not attuned to current events and had no idea that when they chose his first name, they had doomed him to a lifetime of stupid jokes and vague references to his name-sake, one of the greatest and most famous chief justices in the history of the United States Supreme Court. He was not named after this great historical figure.

He was named after Uncle Earl.

Of course, Earl felt curious, if not obligated, to learn about the man for whom so many people thought he was named. His studies into biographies and other books led him to a deep appreciation of the traditions of the law, and the importance of law to many fields of endeavor. The law was everywhere. He found himself drawn to the law with almost mystical reverence. Great debates of morality and the nature of the human condition took place before courts of law throughout history. Lawyers and judges were part of a mahogany-laced netherworld where truth and justice did battle against the forces of evil.

So he was understandably anxious when he arrived at the courthouse several weeks later for his first court appearance. But as he drew nearer to the nondescript building in which his justice was to be dispensed, he felt a vague sense of disappointment. He had never been to a court of law and was expecting more than the simple, bland structure that looked more like a high school than a courthouse that greeted him. He walked slowly up the steps and reached for the handle of the door, passing into the cool interior of the building and beyond the reach of the sweltering Florida sun.

The Deep South high-school type of architectural design had also been adopted for the interior of the building, which consisted of the customary long interconnected hallways and terrazzo floors that are so familiar to the minions of students and teachers who have survived the Florida school system.

Once inside Earl could feel the pulse of humanity all around him. The unassuming exterior of the building had given no hint of the nervous energy housed within the walls of this would-be high school. People walked briskly past him and down the hall with their files and papers. Most bore serious or thoughtful expressions on their faces, hardly noticing Earl as he slowly made his way down the corridor and into a central reception area where he sat down on a bench and took out the summons he had received. He looked at the paper again to be certain he was in the right place, even though he had scrutinized the worn, tattered paper so much he had virtually memorized every word and symbol that appeared on it.

He was trying to fit in in unfamiliar surroundings. Earl's eyes wandered upward and across the reception area to two men in suits engrossed in conversation. He wondered about the topic of their conversation and imagined what their lives were like, spent there every day at the courthouse. Today may have been some sort of plea bargain for a mass murderer. Other days they may discuss more mundane cases, such as an armed robbery or maybe an escape from prison. Earl didn't stop to consider that he was in the section of the courthouse complex where little misdemeanor cases and silly traffic cases such as his were being heard.

Earl surveyed the other people walking through the reception area. Standing near the information counter was a sheriff's deputy, engaged in light banter with a courthouse clerk who sat behind the counter. He watched the portly deputy break out into a soft laughter as the clerk slapped him gently on the shoulder and smiled. They worked every day at the courthouse. They felt quite at home, having long since taken the imposing aura Earl felt for granted. Mixed in with the men and women in suits, the clerks and the deputies, all of whom were at ease in their environment, were the common folk, dressed in casual clothing or conspicuous in their infrequently worn Sunday go-to-meetin' wear, anxious to make the right impression when their cases were called.

Earl himself had spent quite some time thinking about what he should wear. He had decided to wear the uniform of Publix Supermarkets where he worked as a bag boy: plain slacks and plain shirt complemented by a plain tie. He wanted to impress upon the judge that he was really a responsible young man with a steady job at a respectable company. He had even brought his name tag to wear just in case the judge missed the point.

Of course, it was his day off.

When he began to feel uncomfortable just sitting there for no apparent reason, Earl stood up and proceeded down the hall towards the courtroom where he was to make his case to the judge, checking his tattered paper one last time just to make sure. As he walked down the hallway, he wondered why he didn't feel nervous. He was waiting for that gut-wrenching feeling he got every time he had to appear in public and make a speech or something. He knew that when the time came so would the butterflies, but for the moment he felt oddly at ease, obscure among the crowd of people gradually massing near the courtroom entrance.

Earl bent down to take a quick sip of water from the water fountain. He looked up at the clock on the wall. He had only a few minutes to show time, and he still did not feel nervous.

But then again, he wasn't particularly thirsty either.

He knew he was just expending a little nervous energy, trying to pretend as though he naturally belonged there. *What, ME worry? I do this all the time*, he thought to himself.

As the appointed hour approached, the nervous chatter that had filled the hallway began to subside. People began to file solemnly through the entrance to the courtroom. Sitting in the back row, Earl was surprised at the splendor of the courtroom, complete with high ceiling and the customary long aisle leading to the mounted bench behind which the judge would dispense justice. The regal décor of the large room was quite a contrast to the rest of the building.

The nervous chatter of the people assembled together had been replaced by nervous whispers murmuring in the courtroom. A bond had been formed among these strangers even though they said next to nothing to one another. They had all been thrown together in unfamiliar territory to face a common threat and instinctively felt a common kinship. Earl found himself thinking about the scene in the *Wizard of Oz* when the frightened group of adventurers faced the great and powerful Oz. He could sense the unspoken bonding as he exchanged nervous glances with others in the row of seats but then began to draw inward.

Earl was just going over, once again, the speech he had prepared for the judge when he was rudely brought back to reality by the sound of a hundred people clambering to their feet. The din of the masses responding to the cry of the bailiff's "ALL RISE" drowned out the introduction of the judge as he made his grand entrance. By this time the sickening feeling began to gurgle up from the pit of Earl's stomach.

He was too numb with the growing sense of anxiety to pay attention to what the judge was saying during his introductory remarks. Then the court clerk began to call people forward.

Earl's thoughts traveled back to speech class in high school when he used to wait in dread for his name to be called by the teacher when it was his turn to deliver his speech. He would constantly debate whether he should volunteer first and get it over with or experience the brief feeling of euphoria when someone else's name was called instead of his, only to be replaced by fear as the student finished the speech and the time came for the teacher to say those two dreaded words.

"Earl Warren!"

The words broke into his thoughts. They were spoken by the bailiff, who was craning his neck, peering into the audience.

"Are you sure you have that name right?" Earl heard the judge ask as he scrambled to his feet and made his way down the long path to the bench. He felt a hundred pair of eyes on him. He moved as if in a dream to meet his fate, standing awkwardly before the judge, who peered down at him from on high. All thoughts of a prepared speech quickly vanished.

"Well, now, I never thought I would have the pleasure of meeting the Honorable Earl Warren in the flesh," said the judge with a kindly smile. His grandfatherly features made him appear as if he were cast in the role of judge for some Hollywood movie. "I note that the officer who issued the citation is not present in the court today," said the judge as he began sifting through some papers in front of him. "How do you plead, young man?"

"Guilty," said a voice Earl scarcely recognized as his own.

The judge looked up from his paperwork with surprise. "Son, I appreciate your honesty. Normally, this offense calls for a $100 fine. But in your case, I am reducing the fine in half, plus court costs. Next case, please."

Earl shuffled dumbfounded to waiting court clerks who led him like a blind man to a table set up to complete forms to make arrangements for processing the cases and paying the fines. He filled out the forms absent-mindedly, barely able to respond to the simple questions of the clerks, who seemed to delight in his stupor. They had witnessed these experiences many times in the past and were amused at the befuddled looks of their patrons.

Earl made his way out of the courtroom, through the hall, and back into the Florida sunshine. He had just begun to wonder what the judge meant about his honesty. Years would pass before he would learn what the judge meant. Officers, for one reason or another, fail to appear in court. When that happens, knowledgeable defendants plead not guilty (even if they are guilty as sin) and move to dismiss the case for lack of prosecution, seeing as how the government has no evidence and thus no case with which to proceed. Usually the judge will dismiss the case.

Earl had no knowledge of these unwritten rules of the law in traffic court. To him, he was simply guilty and told the judge the truth. His honest approach was so out of place that the judge was moved to show compassion for that reason alone. Earl was perplexed that honesty wasn't taken for granted in a court of law. He had a lot to learn. In a court of law the object is to *win at all costs*, not reach a just and honorable outcome.

Going to court was not quite what Earl expected for many reasons, although he was not sure what to expect. His imagination had run wild, fed by television programs and books on celebrated cases. But even though his first court experience was not as glamorous as he imagined, his dream of becoming a lawyer was not diminished.

In years to come, he would look back on this day and realize the irony of his experience.

But at the time he emerged from that courtroom, Earl was more determined than ever to pursue his dream. Soon he would begin his undergraduate studies. If his grades were good enough, he could start his real education, starting with law school.

CHAPTER II

CUT TO: FOUR YEARS LATER

Pen in mouth, Earl sat staring absently at the swirls of smoke twisting towards the ceiling in the "smoking room" of the law library. He didn't smoke, but the smoking room was a comforting enclave from the rows of students deep in concentration and the deathly silence pervading the main part of the library where the air of fear and tension was almost palpable. Besides, those who chose the smoking room as their study area had formed an informal clique in which the monotony of studying was broken by occasional outbursts of conversation that would be otherwise strictly forbidden on the "outside."

As usual, Earl's mind had traveled far afield to escape the dry text to which he was chained for the afternoon. He had never quite grown accustomed to the peculiar writing style of judges and legal scholars, made up of analytical phrases strung together in logical sequence yet leaving the normal reader baffled. To make matters worse, law school texts are not like other books. The author merely assembles a series of opinions written by judges in selected cases. These opinions are followed by a series of questions meant to stimulate thought as to the meaning of the preceding words of wisdom.

No answers to these questions are provided.

The first day Earl sat down with great anticipation to read one of these books, he thought he would just read a few chapters while waiting for Marilyn at a beauty salon. He had been waiting for this day for a long time, ever since he read a book about the exploits of F. Lee Bailey called *The Defense Never Rests*. He knew after reading that book that someday he would become a lawyer. Now he was about to embark upon the road that would lead him to his lifelong ambition.

But when he opened the book entitled *Criminal Law* (one of his favorite subjects), he found himself aimlessly reading the same words several times, going back to discover what he had missed when his mind began to wander. Flipping forward, he saw the rhetorical questions at the end of each case and noticed that there were no explanations, much less answers to the questions. He eventually put the book down in disgust.

"This *is* English, isn't it?" he said to Marilyn, motioning to the offending book as she emerged from the salon. She gave him a sidelong glance and smile, knowing that he would have little reverence, or patience, with the formalities and rigid language of what was the chosen field for both of them. Then she stopped short, hands on hips, looking at him with disapproval.

"Well?" she said impatiently.

After a moment's hesitation Earl quickly realized the error of his ways. "You look wonderful," he said. "No, wait." He stopped her as she began to turn away. "You look ravishing." With that, he took her in his arms and bent her over backwards, leaning forward to kiss her.

"Earl, please!" she nearly screamed, half laughing. "I just had my hair done."

Earl couldn't help but smile as he recalled this incident. He looked over at Marilyn, who was deep in thought as she read her law book and notes, highlighter poised over the pages. She curled some of her long hair behind her ear and seemed to sense his gaze upon her, glancing at him briefly with a warm smile, her eyes barely disengaging from her studies.

He had met her during his undergraduate studies in one of those rare occasions when the paths of a business student and English major crossed. Although hers was the realm of subjective appreciation of art and his of more precise mathematical calculations, they were drawn to one another. He admired her for her unassuming intelligence and her ability to succeed. She even scored higher than he did on a final exam in an economics class they both had taken. She told him that after taking the test, she did not really understand any of the basic concepts that were taught.

"See, that just proves that what you know or understand is not important in college. You know a lot more about economics than I do. But I scored higher. You just have to know how to take tests," she explained with a shrug.

Earl always wondered if she really meant that or if she thought she had to soothe his ego. Regardless of what she did or didn't retain about economics, Marilyn had, unlike Earl, quickly mastered the techniques needed to excel in law school. Perhaps because of her earlier studies of sometimes obscure literary works, she quickly deciphered the code contained in the law books that only judges, lawyers, and law professors are supposed to understand.

Forcing otherwise ordinary citizens who enter law school to assimilate these textbooks and understand the "code" is part of the grand design of legal education – or to be more precise, legal indoctrination. This process of indoctrination is complemented by the Socratic teaching method. In this method the professor asks questions of a student as to the meaning of a case that had been assigned for that day. Students, who are already insecure at the thought that their fellow classmates with whom they must compete had to be at the top of their undergraduate class in order to get into law school in the first place, live in daily fear that their name will be called in class the next day to face ridicule, or adulation, depending on whether they can answer the question to the satisfaction of the presiding professor.

In short, contrary to popular mythology, law schools do not really teach the law, although the essence of the law is explained to students. The primary purpose of law school is to teach students how to "think like a lawyer." Compassion and "gut reactions" that an ordinary, properly well-adjusted person feels when confronted by a given situation is wrung out of the successful law student and replaced by the peculiar logic of the law that so confounds ordinary citizens.

This is why what to lawyers is elementary, the public often finds absurd or downright outrageous.

The process of indoctrination is reinforced by the competitive environment nurtured by the law school. Those who quickly learn to "think like a lawyer" have an advantage over those who cling to their outmoded ideas of morality and common sense. Marilyn had quickly adapted to the indoctrination method and thrived in law school, while Earl languished.

Coincidentally, most of the chain-smoking inhabitants of the smoking room were at the top of their class and members of the elite law review. Although a regular in this retreat, Earl had not ascended to these upper echelons of the law school. He had foolishly clung to the vagaries of common sense and common decency and had apparently failed to learn how to think properly.

Once, confounded by a grade he received in torts, he visited the professor and asked to see the final exam of the top student in the class. In law school the grade you receive on the final exam given at the end of the semester is the grade you receive for the course.

Professor Wilson greeted him at the door of his office with a somewhat perplexed look on his face.

"Oh, Mr. Justice Warren, please come in," he finally said with a smile. Earl rolled his eyes upward and nodded. He had heard more vague references to his namesake in the past three months than he had heard in his entire life.

Wilson was essentially bald and sported a full, white mustache, which, if he had taken to wearing a top hat and tuxedo, would have given him the appearance similar to the cartoon character that appears on the game board and "Community Chest" cards of Monopoly. Wilson always had a faraway look in his eyes as if he was perpetually seeing visions, or listening to some inner voices.

The first day of class, he entered the room and began to give massages to some of the students. He then explained his theory of the law of torts, which was based upon his belief in reincarnation and a metaphysical view of a unifying life force. But as bizarre as his theories were, Wilson was one of the few professors that emphasized the practical side of the law. A practicing personal injury attorney for many years, he began teaching torts in reverse order, starting with the issue of the damages that were caused to the plaintiff, instead of the legal basis for bringing a suit on behalf of the plaintiff, which is the normal starting point in torts.

"What difference does it make if your client has a legal right to recover?" he explained. "You will be paid based upon a percentage of the damages collected. If there are no damages or the damages don't amount to much, your client isn't going to collect anything, and neither will you, will you? That is why damages is the first and most important issue to consider."

Wilson led Earl to a stack of exams and picked out the one that had received the highest score. As he read it, Earl tried to identify some brilliant idea or insightful passage that made the exam exceptional. But the more he read, the more he felt disappointed. The exam was not exceptional. In fact, it was not too different from his.

Am I missing something? he thought to himself.

"Professor Wilson, I've read this exam, and to be honest with you, I don't understand why this exam received the highest grade in the class. Why did you like it so much?"

"I don't know. I just liked it," he said with a shrug.

As he left Wilson's office, Earl thought about the old adage that law school exams were graded by throwing the papers up a staircase. The one landing nearest the top of the stairs received an "A," with the remaining grades determined in descending order based upon the position of the exam on the staircase. Whoever thought up this adage was as perplexed as Earl was at the seemingly arbitrary way in which grades are given out in law school. But as arbitrary as the system seemed, certain people always did well, and since grades were given on a "blind" grading system, whereby the professor is supposedly unaware of the identity of the author of a given paper, there had to be some method to this madness.

Earl's thoughts were interrupted when Mark began talking aloud in the smoking room to no one in particular, as if he were finishing an earlier conversation.

"You know, I was reading the other day somewhere about how some of the students at Harvard Law School started this ritual in their classes called 'Turkey Bingo.'"

"Turkey Bingo?" asked Earl, relieved at some conversation.

Mark was another exemplary student who had made law review but, like many smoking room regulars, had managed to retain some semblance of proportion, not to mention his sense of humor. As he spoke the corners of his mouth rose in an impish smirk under his dark mustache.

"Yeah. Someone picks the names of certain students and arranges them on a sort of bingo card that is distributed to the class. When each student rises to answer a question, a chip is placed over that student's name. When a student had enough chips in a row, instead of shouting 'bingo,' he or she would have to respond to whatever question had been asked by the professor by using an example involving a turkey."

"What will those brilliant minds at Harvard think of next?" said Marilyn sarcastically. "You're just envious at the obvious heightened awareness of tradition at one of our rival institutions," Mark said as his smirk grew to a wide grin.

"Yeah, they're just looking behind their backs, feeling our hot breath as we pass them in tradition and stature," replied Marilyn, turning back to her studies.

"I don't know, Marilyn. Just because we are a state school in the Deep South doesn't mean those blue bloods have anything over on us," Earl said. Marilyn ignored him. "In fact, I think I'm going to start our own Turkey Bingo tradition." As he rose to leave, Marilyn just looked at him and smiled, before going back to her studies.

When he got home, Earl dug out the "yearbook" that had been given to each entering freshman. Pictures of his classmates were printed on the handout. He held it in one hand, scissors in the other, pausing for a moment.

Someday, twenty years from now, I could be holding this in my hand, thinking about the good old days of law school, he thought to himself. *If I slice this up now, I may never forgive myself.*

"Ah, the sacrifices one must make for tradition," he said aloud as he began to cut out the pictures of the students that he knew were the most vocal in class. Behind each cut-out he put a piece of tape. Then he prepared a game card with blank spaces arranged in rows and instructions on how to play. Then he went to the library copy machine, making several versions of the game cards by rearranging the pictures in the blank spaces.

When word got out about the game, Earl was flooded with so many requests for game cards, he had to charge students to cover his copy expenses. Some people bought several cards, presumably to increase their odds. Earl got the idea that maybe some of them just wanted a memento.

That afternoon, Earl sat outside on a bench, reading a *Case Notes* for an upcoming constitutional law class. *Case Notes* gave a capsule summary of each case in the chosen textbook of the class and offered analysis of the points of law which the case was intended to represent.

Another study aid is *Gilberts*, which consists of an explanatory outline of a subject.

Study aids such as *Case Notes* and *Gilberts* attempt to fill the void created by the case method and Socratic teaching by giving a straightforward explanation of what the law is. Some enterprising former law student who found an easier way to make a living than practicing law probably developed them. But while a godsend to panic-stricken law students, the study guides are the bane of law professors. Any self-respecting professor will quickly humiliate a student caught with the offending books in his class as a way of demonstrating the limited utility of such crib notes in the genuine understanding of a subject as complex as the law.

Like most other law students, Earl relied upon the quick information provided by the study aids. But *Case Notes*, in particular, was essential for him since he could not afford to purchase all of the textbooks required for his classes. He was reading the *Case Notes* for "con law" (another favorite subject) just in case he was questioned on the holding of a particular case when he heard the sound of boots on the pavement approaching him. When he looked up, Becky had already reached where he was sitting, one boot resting up on the seat of the bench, her hand on her knee. She was wearing her customary tight jeans and leathers.

Becky was a biker.

"So, I hear you have this thing going for contracts class. Mind filling me in?" She looked at him with a sly grin.

Putting his *Case Notes* away, Earl pulled out a bingo card. "Well, I guess I can take a break from my intense studying," he replied, returning her smile. She sat down next to him as he explained the game to her. She nodded her head in approval and got up to go back to her own studying.

"Wait a second, what's going on to change the helmet laws?" Earl also rode a motorcycle and knew she was lobbying to have the mandatory helmet laws repealed.

"Right now it looks like we're going to go down to utter defeat, as usual. But, you know, I did get a chance to talk to Professor Whittaker at the last keg party about that decision on the helmet law when he was still sitting on the Supreme Court." Whittaker was a retired judge who taught civil procedure at the law school. He had written an opinion upholding the constitutionality of the helmet laws.

"He was actually pretty apologetic," she said. "He told me the other judges didn't care enough about the issue to even write an opinion. They just wanted to affirm the lower court without explanation. But he really agonized over the constitutional issues, even though he ended up ruling against the right to ride without a helmet."

"So you've forgiven him?" asked Earl, who knew better.

"Wait 'til we have the professor's auction," she said with a smile. "I'm going to bid on his offer to spend a full day with any student and make him do my laundry."

Earl watched as she walked away. He was comforted to know that there were other people in law school who retained their individuality through the process of indoctrination. He was about to go back to his studying when he saw Marilyn across the plaza. When she caught his eye, she motioned to him, walked over, and took a seat next to him.

"Hard at work studying again, I see," she said as she gently rubbed her hand across his back.

He just looked across at her and smiled warmly.

"You know, Marilyn, I don't think I'm going to get a high enough grade point average after this semester to make law review."

"You have to study harder, Earl."

"But it's not that I don't understand the material; I just don't seem to be able to write the type of final exam that the professors are looking for. How do you do it?"

She studied him for a short while. She had been ranked high enough after her first two semesters of law school to be invited to join the law review. The point of law review was not that writing stale articles on obscure legal issues was stimulating. Those students that are part of law review are heavily recruited by law firms and Supreme Court justices, ensuring a well-paying place in the legal establishment. The rest of the law school class had to scramble for any job they could find in a market teeming with would-be lawyers.

"You are probably one of the most intelligent people in this law school, Earl," she said, looking into his eyes. "And I know you can write well. I can't exaplain why you haven't gotten higher grades on your exams, but you also have to understand that you have gotten higher grades on some of your exams than most of the people in your class. Your GPA is almost high enough to get you into law review. But if you don't make it next semester, you can always try to write-on."

"Writing-on" is where the law review allows any student to submit a paper on a recent case.

If the paper is good enough, the student is invited to join law review.

"Thanks, Marilyn," Earl said, reaching for her hand. "I'll give it my best shot."

The next day the class was murmuring with anticipation before contracts class. Earl walked in at the top of the room to take his customary seat in the back of the class. The room had been designed as a sort of an amphitheater, with the seats arranged in rows up a steep incline that curved in a half circle around the center podium, where the professor gave his lecture. From his perch at the top and back of the room, Earl looked down at his colleagues, most of whom had Turkey Bingo cards amidst their notes and textbooks scattered before them on their desks.

Earl descended to the podium to address the class.

"Does anyone have any last minute questions before we begin the first annual session of Turkey Bingo?"

"Yeah. How will you prevent cheating?" someone called out.

"I have a strict monitoring system that ensures compliance." He lied, as he had no way of knowing if the declared winner had cheated.

"What does the winner get?" someone else asked.

"The admiration of his peers. Besides, I'm not sure if giving a prize would be legal."

At that moment Professor Hughs entered the room. Earl quickly made his way back to his seat as the class quieted down. The lecture proceeded as usual. Hughs was a thin man in his forties with lightly graying hair. As he spoke, he had a nervous habit of interrupting his sentences with a throat-clearing sound that he made as he brought his fist to his mouth. As the discussion became livelier, his throat-clearing would rise to a fever pitch, punctuating his words in machine-gun fashion.

The lecture dragged on for nearly the entire hour. Earl kept glancing at the clock, wondering if the class would end without a Turkey Bingo champion.

"Assume that the farmer in this example did not produce the number of eggs called for in his agreement -ahem- because of, let's say, a disease that affected his brood. Could he claim impossibility of performance as a defense to breach of contract?" Hughs asked, continuing with the example he had been using for the last few minutes to illustrate a point.

Steve Hardy raised his hand and stood to answer the question. He was tall and sported a full, red beard that gave him a striking appearance.

He was another biker.

"He may be able to claim impossibility, but the answer would depend on the terms of the contract. He might also be able to claim mitigation of damages as a defense if he made up some of the losses by selling some assets if, for example, the holiday season was approaching and the other party agreed to accept a brood of turkeys from the farmer's adjacent turkey farm."

At that, the class burst into uncontrolled laughter and then a sustained applause, as Hardy gave a slight bow and sat down. Hughs, unaware of what was happening, was attempting to respond to Hardy's reply through the din. As he continued to incorporate the turkey farm example into his lecture in-between accelerating throat-clearings, the class continued to chuckle.

Earl sat in the back of the class smiling broadly. The whole exercise had been a greater success than he had expected.

Turkey Bingo would prove to be the highlight of his law school experience.

CHAPTER III
THE BLACK LETTER OF THE LAW

Earl was so engrossed in the book he was reading on the couch in the smoking room that he didn't notice Marilyn had walked into the room.

"What are you doing?" she asked after a while as she stood in front of him. "Oh, hi. I didn't see you walk in."

"Final exams are only three weeks away. Don't you think you should start studying?"

"I am studying."

"That doesn't look like a law book to me."

Earl looked at the paperback he had been reading. The book was a recently released expose' on the inner workings of the Supreme Court, an institution shrouded in mystery. By revealing the backdoor lobbying and bitter philosophical feuds among the justices, the authors had provided an insight into the decisions studied by Earl and his fellow students that they could never have attained by reading law texts.

The book was particularly critical of Chief Justice Moorehead, who was portrayed as a pompous, manipulative man of questionable scholastic background that had cynically turned one of the most important institutions of constitutional government into his own private political playground.

"I'll have you know that this book is virtually required reading for con law in Stevens' class," he said as he waved the book in the air. "He spends more of his time in class talking about this book than he does the opinions. Reading it will give me an insight into how the man thinks."

He looked up at her sheepishly, as she glared at him with mock indignation. She quickly swiveled and sat down next to him, snatching the book from his hands, leafing through the pages with an occasional "um-hum" and glance in his direction. With her body pressed up close against his, all thoughts of philosophical feuds vanished. All he could think about was the tingling sensation rippling through his body and the smell of her perfume.

"I've heard several people complain about Stevens," she said, turning to him slightly. "They felt they hadn't really learned too much about constitutional law. Others I've heard about said he was a wonderful teacher. I guess it all depends on the individual." With that she rose from the couch and settled down to her own studying.

Earl looked at her, frowning briefly. Then he looked down at his book, thinking of Professor Stevens. Stevens was unlike most law school professors. He was probably in his late forties, but with his thin red beard and blue jeans that he wore to class, he could have easily passed for a man in his thirties, a holdover from the Vietnam War and the radical sixties. One day he showed up in class still wearing his helmet, apparently having commuted that day on a motorcycle.

Early in that first semester, Stevens stunned the class by explaining that the United States Constitution was technically never legally ratified as required under the Articles of Confederation, the predecessor to the current Constitution. He then spent most of the semester espousing a theory that the Constitution was a collection of abstract principles interpreted by the Supreme Court in accordance with the mix of political ideology embraced by the justices sitting on the Court at any particular moment in history.

He likened the Court to a "super legislature" that passes upon the great issues of society with only minimal reference to the text of the Constitution. When the prevailing votes on the Court were more conservative in outlook, individual rights were diminished while rights of property were more frequently upheld against governmental interference.

To illustrate this point, he would draw a graph on the blackboard showing that in the late 1930s, when the conservative Court struck down liberal New Deal legislation, protection of property rights reached a zenith, only to swing to the opposite end of the political spectrum after the Court-packing plan of President Roosevelt in 1937, and the subsequent rise of the more liberal Court of Chief Justice Earl Warren.

As proof of his faith in more conventional methods of expressing the political will of the people, Professor Stevens adopted an unusual grading method for the class. The students were asked to propose and then vote upon the distribution of grades for the course. There was a rumor on campus that a previous class voted to give every student a "B," except those who had utterly failed on the final exam who would receive an "E." The administration was said to be so outraged that they figured the grades for that class on a pass-fail basis.

On the day that Earl's class was to vote on their own grading curve, Andrew Harvey, one of the more ambitious students of the class, raised his hand and asked if Stevens would honor any vote by the students, even one which gave every student an "A." Stevens looked at him and hesitated momentarily, stroking his beard. There was no doubt he would abide by any wish of the collective body, or so he taught.

Another, older student then spoke. He said that such a grading scale would be unfair to those students who had studied hard to understand the complex constitutional issues that had been discussed during the semester. Stevens again said nothing. He then looked up at the class and announced that he would leave the room so as to not influence the final outcome.

When Stevens left, there was very little debate. Even Andrew Harvey relented under the weight of opinion that the class should vindicate the professor's idealistic faith in the democratic process. Earl rose and suggested that the class adopt a standard "bell curve" that distributed grades under a commonly-used statistical standard deviation. The suggestion was adopted, and the class called Stevens in to inform him of the results of their vote.

He just nodded and continued with the lecture.

After class Earl saw Stevens in the hallway, cornered by a group of students. As he approached the group, he overheard a question by one student concerning the blind grading system.

"There is no blind grading system," Stevens replied to a stunned silence. "Despite what you may have heard, professors have access to the names of students whose papers they are grading if they choose to do so, and most do. How do you think they submit grades to the administration? At some point someone has to transfer the grades from the Social Security numbers on your exams to report cards. The blind grading myth is a hoax to keep students from feeling that certain students are given special treatment over others."

Earl just looked on, dumbfounded at this revelation.

A few days later, Stevens had the class vote on subjects to be discussed during the semester since the material was too vast to cover every aspect of this area of the law adequately in the time allowed. A student active in the women's movement spoke up and asked that we cover abortion. Another student suggested that we cover discrimination laws. As each suggestion was made, Stevens dutifully wrote them on the chalkboard.

Earl finally raised his hand and was recognized. "Death penalty," he deadpanned.

Stevens stiffened for a moment as he considered the proposed topic. He was known to be an ardent opponent of the death penalty. Yet polls indicated an overwhelming number of people in favor of it. Earl wondered how Stevens, as a staunch defender of majority rule, could oppose the imposition of a penalty that the public supported in such great numbers.

Earl himself had come to the conclusion that the death penalty was perfectly justified, although he had never been confronted by anyone of a contrary view. Any person who had such total disregard for human life deserved like treatment. There is little room in such a harsh world of sometimes brutal, yet expedient, measures to consider, let alone implement, such a quaint notion as mercy, even where human life is at stake.

Stevens wrote "Death Penalty" on the blackboard along with the other topics. As he pointed to each one, the class voted by a show of hands. "Death Penalty" was approved overwhelmingly by the students. After the tally Stevens seemed to draw himself together, bracing himself for the fierce task that lay before him.

The first order of business was to read the Constitution itself. The Fifth Amendment clearly alludes to "capital" crimes, provides that no person can be twice placed in jeopardy of "life," and states that no person can be deprived of "life" unless given due process of law, a phrase that is repeated in the Fourteenth Amendment. The people who wrote the Bill of Rights therefore clearly had no doubt as to the constitutionality of the death penalty.

But the Fifth Amendment also states that no person can be twice put in jeopardy of "life" (or limb) and, although at the time the Constitution was ratified, the practice of branding and ear cropping for criminals was common, physical mutilation is too barbarous even for the most conservative justices of the Court (or at least most of them) to accept.

So much of the debate over whether the death penalty is "cruel and unusual" punishment and, therefore, unconstitutional under the Eighth Amendment has focused on whether the public has evolved into a sufficiently civilized society so as to abhor such primitive and brutal sanctions. The discussion in Stevens' class then proceeded to the two justifications upon which the weight of public opinion determined that the country had not yet reached a stage of enlightenment where society felt uncomfortable with allowing the government to terminate the lives of its citizens: deterrence and retribution.

Stevens produced statistical studies showing that the death penalty does not deter crime. These studies were supported by others of a more general nature which have established that the swiftness and certainty of punishment has a much greater effect on crime than the severity of the punishment. Unless society was prepared to accept summary trials and executions with little or no avenue of appeal, the remoteness and uncertainty of a death sentence will realistically never deter a person in a given situation from murder. Besides which, most murders were crimes of passion which are not conducive to reflection or consideration of consequences that may result years later.

Returning to his more customary premise of government and constitutional law, Stevens then pointed out that of the 70-some-odd percent of those in favor of the death penalty, about 40 percent stated that they would not support the death penalty if it was proved not to be a deterrent. Another 30-or-so percent also indicated that they would favor abolition of death sentences if the offenders were given life without possibility of parole. When taken into consideration these factors undercut the argument that the government had the blessing of most people in carrying out executions and that society had not yet evolved to the point of rejecting the ultimate penalty.

But the logic of these arguments did not convince most of the class members. Andrew Harvey spoke up and made the point that the death penalty at the very least did deter the person executed from committing future crimes, a concept known as "specific deterrence." He also argued that even if there was only a single person deterred from committing murder because of the fear of a death sentence that would justify it.

Stevens responded that life without possibility of parole also prevented the accused from committing further crimes without going to the extreme of killing that person. He then offered a startling counter-argument to Harvey's other point.

There have been a number of documented instances where murders had been committed precisely because the murderer wanted to receive the death penalty. This phenomenon is known as the "death wish syndrome." Stevens showed that even if a limited general deterrent effect could be proved, this effect was far outweighed by the known effect of the death penalty that actually *caused* people to commit murder.

Stevens next brought in a history professor who traced the death penalty, at least in the South, to Jim Crow laws and the torture/hangings of people of color during a lynching. Thought to be a thing of the distant past, Earl was stunned to learn that lynching was still taking place in the early part of the 20th century. These revelations, together with still more statistical evidence showing the death penalty inflicted the ultimate penalty disproportionately on people of color, painted a picture of a gruesome practice visited primarily on minorities and the poor.

Still, most students could not rid themselves of the instinctive reaction to the heinous crimes committed by those who sat on death row. Some even suggested that the taxpayers should not have to be forced to pay to have these people remain in prison. But Stevens showed that the cost of carrying out an execution is comparable, if not more than, the expense incurred to house these inmates in prison.

But the crux of the death penalty debate in Stevens' class came down to emotion, not analysis. The same seemed to be true in the Supreme Court, which ultimately held that imposition of the death penalty was not cruel and unusual punishment. The Court even held as part of its reasoning that society had the right to satisfy the desire to see perpetrators die for their crimes, and if the courts did not allow the satisfaction of this desire, the judiciary would fall into disrepute, and citizens would begin to take the law into their own hands.

No amount of studies and analysis could refute the basic notion that the death penalty provided an outlet for the public which demanded the blood of murderers in retribution for the crimes they have committed. American society as a whole wanted an eye for an eye, not to turn the other cheek.

Almost all of the countries in western civilization have abandoned the death penalty. Even Nazi war criminals guilty of mass murder on a scale that the most ambitious sociopath in modern society could not attain have been given mercy from this most final and brutal of punishments. The people of the United States have not evolved to this level as of yet, and so the death penalty will continue to be imposed.

Earl was profoundly affected by the debate over the death penalty in Stevens' class. When he talked to Marilyn about what had transpired in class, she kidded him about how he had finally found a topic in law school that held his interest. She was far more comfortable with professors who relied upon "black letter law," where rules and basic principles are learned and then applied to a given factual scenario. The adherents to this view of the law were not interested in some fancy theory of human behavior or public policy, much less subjects and analysis with such latent moral and philosophical undertones that inevitably crept up in constitutional law.

With these thoughts Earl looked over again at Marilyn who was, as usual, concentrating on her studies. *How ironic*, he thought to himself. After years of studying the abstractions inherent in literature and learning to analyze and critique the subjective, Marilyn demanded, and thrived upon, order and logic in the study of law while disdaining the more amorphous theories upon which the law and government itself are based.

CHAPTER IV
BACK TO THE FUTURE

Earl made his way around to the driver's side door of Marilyn's candy-apple red Firebird, after putting their cooler and other accessories in the back of the car. As he slid behind the wheel, he cast a sheepish smile in her direction. He felt self-conscious driving around in such a flashy car, especially with a beautiful woman in the passenger seat. She didn't seem to notice his look.

She was staring aimlessly out the window, her head reclined, letting the morning sun flicker on her face through the open window as he pulled out into the street.

The stress and strain of final exams was finally over, to be replaced with anticipation, if not dread, at the final outcome of the semester they both had just completed. Marilyn had until the following day before her flight left for her home in Miami. She quickly agreed to Earl's suggestion that they drive to the beach for the day to relax before her trip.

"Well?" she said, finally breaking the silence. She tilted her head slightly in his direction, looking at him through her dark sunglasses. "Did you make it?"

Earl blew out a burst of air and shrugged. "Who knows, Marilyn. These tests are so arbitrary. Of course, I know I did well in con law." He looked at her with a sly grin.

She adjusted herself in her seat. "I'm sure. But what about your other exams?"

"I think I did reasonably well on all of them. But to make law review, I would have had to have aced just about all of those exams, and I have a feeling I didn't quite manage that."

They continued driving along for a while in silence. Then Marilyn reached forward to open the sunroof door. She adjusted her chair and her position so that the sunlight drenched her torso. Earl kept glancing over, eyeing her bulging breasts barely harnessed by her swimsuit. He caught her eye as he looked up, smiling weakly.

"I guess I might as well start working on my vacation total tan," she said with a mischievous grin. With that, she unhooked the top of her swimsuit, unleashing her breasts with a jiggle and a broad grin in Earl's direction.

The car immediately swerved back into their lane with a jerk as Earl quickly brought his attention from Marilyn to the road, straining to look at her out of the corner of his eye and not to be obvious about it. Marilyn laughed.

"Having trouble keeping your eyes on the road, Mr. Chief Justice Warren?" she said as she reclined back in her seat.

He looked at her and raised an eyebrow slightly, as if this were an everyday occurrence. Marilyn was like that: seemingly conservative, even pretentious, but harboring a mischievous ilk towards unconventional, even wild fantasies. For some reason Earl didn't want Marilyn to know that her bare, full breasts, gleaming and swaying in the morning sun were anything but an everyday occurrence for him.

Certainly they were not a cause for arousal.

When they finally got to the beach, Marilyn reattached the top half of her swimsuit, smiling at him wickedly.

"What's the matter? Don't you want to test your right to free speech by exhibiting the female form in all its glory for the rest of the public to see?" Earl asked, sarcastically.

She just looked at him, still smiling, before heading towards the surf.

Earl unloaded the car and settled into a chair, letting the sun wash across his face and body. After a few minutes he sat up, shading his eyes with his hand, as he looked towards the ocean. He made out Marilyn's shapely figure just as she leaped forward and under the advancing waves.

Reaching for the cooler he pulled out a bottle of beer, cracked open the cap, and sat back in his chair with a sigh, looking back out over the waves and the horizon in the distance.

He did not notice the police officer approaching him. "Son, what do you think you're doin'?"

"I'm just sitting here, Officer. What seems to be the problem?"

"That beer is illegal."

"What do you mean?"

"There's an ordinance against having beer or any other alcoholic beverages on the beach. Let me take a look in your cooler."

Earl opened the cooler to reveal another bottle of the offending beverage. The police officer ordered him to throw both bottles into the trash can. Earl complied. He was not about to cause a scene by invoking his constitutional rights over two beers. Run-ins with the police are not good for law students who plan on becoming lawyers. The officer filled out a citation, asking for Earl's name and other information.

"Are you citing me for this?" Earl asked, incredulous. "That's right."

"Look, Officer, I only had two bottles of beer, and I didn't even drink any of it."

The officer eyed him. "Under this ordinance, it's illegal to even possess alcohol regardless of whether you are drunk and disorderly or if you haven't even had a drink. Why, if you had a case of expensive champagne in your trunk, going to some fancy party later, I could cite you for that and confiscate it."

"Don't worry, Officer, you cleaned me out. Two beers is all I have," Earl said with a smile. "But, you know, I have come to this beach many times in the past and have never been cited for drinking beer."

"It's a new law," replied the officer as he tore off the citation and handed it to Earl. "Besides which, ignorance of the law is no excuse." The officer smiled and tipped his hat slightly towards Marilyn as she walked towards them. "Have a nice day, ma'am," he said as he headed back towards his car.

"What happened?" she asked, turning towards Earl with a concerned look.

"Oh, nothing. Just a $50 fine for having a beer on the beach. It's a misdemeanor."

"What?" She just looked at him.

"Don't worry; I'll figure some way out of this."

Marilyn gave him a concerned look. They spent the rest of their time at the beach splashing in the surf and trying to relax in the afternoon sun. But the beer controversy seemed to hang like a cloud over their day at the beach. On the way back, they had driven for several miles before Marilyn spoke up.

"You'll have to report this citation on your application to the bar association, Earl." She looked at him with an expression of total seriousness and concern.

"I know that, but don't you think that this law is a little bit draconian? Anyone with beer or anything else must be strip searched and arrested even if they are not causing a problem – even if they aren't even drinking?"

"I'm just worried about what the bar will think."

"But Marilyn, this doesn't seem fair. He said even if I had a case of expensive champagne in the trunk he could take it and arrest me. Even you would have to object to that." He looked at her as he spoke, regretting his last comment as soon as he said it. She did not seem to notice.

"You didn't provoke him, did you?" she asked, without hesitation. "I know you."

"No, I was very polite, as usual. I even consented to his illegal Fourth Amendment search of my cooler. This is a question of principle, not etiquette. How can we as future lawyers sit back and take such an intrusion on our liberties?"

"Don't get so carried away. You may be more of an expert on con law than I, but as far as I know there is no constitutional right to drink a beer on the beach."

She has a point, he thought to himself.

Earl pushed a CD into the tape player after a few minutes of silence. He knew that Marilyn was just worried about any problems he may have with the bar association. But her worries ran contrary to his strong feelings to challenge what both of them knew to be something that was wrong. As the music rushed over them, she looked at him with a plaintive expression. He smiled and reached around her shoulders, pulling her towards him.

That evening Earl sat at his desk, looking at the paper he had received from the officer. The paper was actually a notice for him to appear in court to plead to the charge of possession of a beer. He went through his textbook on con law and criminal law, trying to find something to help him.

He knew after a short while that he would have to do some extensive research.

The next day at the law library, he wandered through several books leading from possession of illegal substances to alcoholic beverages in general. His research led him to review the history of the era of prohibition.

He found that in the early part of the 20th century, the Temperance League gained in political strength and eventually succeeded in passing the Volstead Act, a law which attempted to enforce prohibition in the United States. The "Great Experiment" of prohibition proved to be so difficult to enforce that the country embarked upon a radical departure from the Constitution by adopting the 18th Amendment to the U.S. Constitution in 1921, which granted to Congress the right to enact legislation to enforce the new moral decree. The only similar sweeping grant of power to Congress in constitutional history was to free the slaves and extend civil liberties to all

American citizens, as provided in the 13th and 14th Amendments to the Constitution.

Earl found that most of the legal history of the prohibition era had been buried deep in the past and forgotten, almost as if the "Great Experiment" had turned into a great mistake. The idea of prohibition, though born of good intentions, ran contrary to many fundamental concepts of American society. American society is premised upon the basic idea that every person may act freely, so long as the exercise of that freedom does not interfere with the rights of others.

Prohibition was a way of "legislating morality" that runs contrary to this basic ideal. Prohibition was so radical a departure from the normal freedoms taken for granted by American citizens that the forces of temperance felt the need to create a vast exception to the Constitution and the Bill of Rights. The result was many cases upholding even the most outrageous of circumstances, all in the interest of breaking the back of "demon rum." Earl tracked down and read one book in particular that details some of the worst cases decided by the courts during prohibition. The book is called *Ill-Starred Prohibition Cases*. Clarence Darrow, probably the greatest lawyer in American history, wrote the following preface to the book in 1931:

> *[T]he courts have stretched and magnified the Eighteenth Amendment and the Volstead*

> *Act until they have destroyed many of the*
> *well established rights of property and per-*
> *sonal freedom, and are fast undermining the*
> *well-established rights won by ages of sacrifice*
> *and human endeavor.*

Earl began to "Shepardize" some of the old prohibition cases in the book and look for modern authority on the subject. "Shepardizing" is named for a research book that refers the reader to all cases that mention the case being Shepardized. If the case was overruled by a later case, or just cited in a footnote, Shepards would give the book and page number of the case where the older case had been discussed.

Earl noticed that a number of the cases in the Clarence Darrow book had been recently used by the Supreme Court to expand the power of the police in pursuing charges under drug laws. Most of these cases gave police greater power to search with or without a warrant, limiting the reach of the Fourth Amendment right to be free from "unreasonable search and seizure."

There was a chilling analogy between prohibition of liquor and that of illegal recreational drugs. In both cases a vast segment of society imbibed the forbidden poison of choice while the government and the proponents of temperance attempted to save these citizens from themselves. The inevitable black market was then created and actually perpetuated by the very illegality that made dealing in contraband economically attractive.

Never in the history of the Constitution had an amendment been repealed. But in 1934, the 18th Amendment to the Constitution, which allowed prohibition, was repealed less than a year after being first sent to the states for ratification by the state convention method. The state convention method of ratifying an amendment to the Constitution allows the people to elect delegates directly, rather than relying upon state legislators, to pass an amendment. This method has only been used once: to repeal prohibition by passing the 21st Amendment.

What a shame we have learned little from prohibition, Earl thought to himself.

But as he read about the assault upon the Constitution so long ago, he thought back to Marilyn's comment. He had been charged with a crime that was reminiscent of a bygone era when basic civil liberties had been discarded in the interest of the more expedient enforcement of laws many people disregarded. Yet he could not place his finger on a single constitutional right that had been violated in his case. He felt an innate instinct that his freedom had been invaded and knew that this law, as written, went too far. But if he could find no legal authority to support his instincts he had no choice but to plead guilty and pay his fine. He knew that history had repeated itself and that in some small way his own experience at the beach was a symptom of what he had grown to suspect was a deterioration of the social and constitutional system of which he was an unwilling part. But with this realization and all that he knew about the subject at hand, he still had no constitutional violation, much less any credible argument to save him from a misdemeanor conviction for possession of a beer on the beach.

Earl sat back and surveyed the opened books and scattered papers on the table in the smoking room. The library was empty except for him, as near as he could tell. Everyone had left for the brief break before classes resumed.

Here I am, contemplating human civilization and how history repeats itself, he thought to himself, *while the rest of civilization is relaxing or spending time with loved ones.*

"Probably having a beer or two to boot," he found himself saying aloud.

He rose from the table in the smoking room and ventured out into the sprawling, empty library. He walked past the stacks of shelves, stroking his chin. He stopped by a set of what are, in essence, legal encyclopedias called *Corpus Juris Secundum* or *CJS* for short. Sitting at a nearby table, he scanned over the sections on "Alcoholic Beverages," paying particular attention to footnotes and an interesting line of cases focusing on the property rights of vendors.

Then he saw it.

In a footnote, the *CJS* referred to a Florida Supreme Court case decided in 1918 that held that a person had a constitutional right to possess booze because booze is property.

"YES!" Earl shouted out loud at the top of his voice. He knew no one would hear him. He ran to the stacks with the volume of the case in the *CJS*. Like all older cases, the language was even more tortured than modern Judge-English, but the implication was clear: the highest court in the state had held, under the *state* constitution, not federal, that a man caught with a fifth of gin in the back seat of his car had a constitutional right to possess that bottle of booze. The court, in a four to three decision, in the midst of prohibition fervor, and despite the fact that three-quarters of the state had already gone dry, held that a law prohibiting the possession of a fifth of gin was unconstitutional because gin is property.

Thank God a majority of the Supreme Court had a snort now and then, even back then, Earl thought as he looked up to the ceiling with a grin, addressing the long dead jurists who had given him new hope on such a seemingly trivial question of law.

Earl was just finishing Shepardizing the case and checking his later authorities to make sure the case had not been overruled or undercut by later decisions when the lights in the library flickered off and on. He felt almost giddy as he gathered his notes and papers. The librarian was quick to lock the door as he strolled out of the library, humming. As he made his way to the parking lot, he noticed Frank Taylor scurrying to catch up to him.

Frank was slightly older than most first-year law students. As with about a quarter of the class, he had pursued a career after graduation from undergraduate college for a few years before entering law school. Tall and thin, he had a ready smile and seemed excited about becoming part of college life again after spending time in "the real world." Frank had a square jaw and a slight dimple in his chin. His features and mannerisms reminded Earl of Ted Turner, the media tycoon.

Earl and Frank felt a sort of kinship. They both were graduates of the business school and enjoyed talking about political philosophies. Frank was trying to reconcile his conservative beliefs on economics with his more liberal views on social issues. Lately, he had become involved in student politics. His brother Fred was recently elected as an official in the student government.

"Just the man I need to see," he said as he drew closer. "I need a con law expert."

"Oh?"

"Yeah, I have a problem I was just researching before they threw me out. Maybe you can help."

"I ordinarily would charge $250 per hour for such advice, but maybe I'll let you slide for a few beers."

"Deal."

They made their way in Frank's car to a small pub in the nearly deserted college town. The pitcher of beer was almost empty by the time they finished trading notes about final exams.

"So what is this problem you are having? You better draw upon my infinite wisdom of constitutional law before we finish this next pitcher," Earl said, pouring the last of the beer into their glasses and nodding towards the waitress looking towards them expectantly. They were the only patrons in the pub.

"Well, as you may have heard, we have been struggling to establish this new political party on campus."

"Frank, I have to be honest with you. I'm not exactly the biggest fan of student politics.

People of my generation are very cynical about the system."

"I know, but, you know, things will never improve if people don't start to get involved.

That's why student government is so screwed up. Students are apathetic."

"No. You have it reversed. Students are apathetic because student government is so screwed up. The student politicians are prima donnas who are only interested in filling up their resumes and practicing to be inept legislators. Even when they show some amount of original thought, the administration will just veto any decision that they make."

"I guess it is natural to be a little cynical."

"I think it goes a lot deeper than that, Frank. Students here are taught not to expect much from their representatives. They are taught that they can't make a difference and to try is just a waste of time. The same is true with the public at large. Every year the turnout rate at election time gets lower and lower. The government is no longer of the people. We are ruled by a group of elites who are teaching future generations to accept that this is the way government operates today."

"But, Earl, in each generation there are people who stand up against the system, and others who work from within to change it. Our political party is different. Our whole platform is based on change of the status quo. That is why we are having problems."

"What kind of problems?"

"Some of the entrenched student government types are trying to limit our campaign activities." Frank pulled out some papers and handed them to Earl. There were copies of letters sent by the student government warning about signs, limits on the amount of time to campaign, and other restrictions.

"I don't think most of this is constitutional," Earl said after looking at the papers. "Of course, I can't represent you in court yet, but I'll help any way I can."

Frank looked at Earl and grinned. Earl lifted his glass and clumsily clinked it against Frank's. "I may be cynical, but I will always defend the Bill of Rights." They had almost finished the second pitcher, and he was starting to slur his words.

"Frank, can I ask you something?"

"What?"

"Has anyone ever told you you look like Ted Turner?"

Frank looked at him with a baffled expression. "No," he said finally. "Why?"

"Never mind."

CHAPTER V
A KING'S RANSOM

Earl walked slowly by the door leading into the offices of the law review, trying to be inconspicuous. He stopped near the bulletin board next to the door, looking around in the hallway self-consciously. He felt uncomfortable at the thought that someone might see him reading the announcement tacked up giving information about "writing on" to the law review.

He was a week into the new semester and had confirmed what he already knew after final exams: he did not make law review. His grades were respectable, but not nearly good enough. Only the top five or six people of the class would be invited to become writers for the elite legal journal that was the stepping stone to success in the profession after graduation.

Although not a rabid over-achiever, Earl did want to do well in law school. He had been disappointed when he saw his grades that were posted along with the others next to his Social Security number, presumably so as to facilitate the "blind grading" system of grading. He was already resigned to the fact that he probably did not make law review, but to face the stark reality on the printed page gave him a momentary twinge of melancholy.

Oh well, life goes on, he thought to himself.

He was not particularly bitter about this milestone he had passed without distinction.

Marilyn was more concerned about his situation than he was. She had made law review and was already an editor. Since she had started a few semesters ahead of Earl, she knew the gauntlet he would run. She gave him advice and information, becoming a sort of mentor. She seemed somewhat distressed, now that her charge had not quite passed the first big hurdle towards success.

The day before, after he had shared the bad news with her, they were in the smoking room.

He was reading over some cases for Frank. She was reading someone's article submitted for publication. Mark had left the smoking room to look up a case, leaving them alone together.

"They posted the list of cases to write on today outside the law review. You should go take a look at them," she said as soon as the door closed behind Mark.

"Do you have to choose one of those cases to write about?"

"You don't have to, but they choose these cases for a reason. The cases usually deal with an important development of the law or a unique fact pattern in a particular case. You can sometimes get an idea of what to write about by looking at the dissents or concurrences of other justices in the case."

"I suppose most of the cases are about boring topics like commercial paper or bank regulations."

Marilyn was not amused. She glared at him for a moment.

"Look, Earl, I'm sorry if you find that legal issues other than con law don't quite suit your fancy. Do you want to try to write on, or do you just want to forget about law review?"

"I'm sorry. I know you're trying to help. I guess I have become a little cynical about law school. I feel as though the grading system is arbitrary and unfair. Some of the people in my class were really crushed about their grades. They're not used to losing. A lot of them are very disenchanted with the system."

"You're right. The system is unfair. But the important thing is that when you get out of law school, the job you get and the amount of money you make depends on the grades you made and things like law review. Don't give up yet."

Earl looked at the earnest expression on Marilyn's face. He knew she was right. He knew she cared about him. He reached out and smoothed her long hair back along the side of her face in a gentle, caressing motion. A smile slowly parted his lips.

"Well, maybe I'll get lucky and there will be a case on freedom of speech or something."

He smiled now as he thought about their conversation in the smoking room. But there were no cases on freedom of speech on the list. One case did look interesting, though. A company had sued to keep the president from transferring billions of dollars to Iran as part of a deal to release hostages made by his predecessor. The Supreme Court sided with the president and upheld the transfer.

Earl took down the citation to the case, taking a last look around to see if anyone had noticed him. He wasn't really sure why he felt so ill at ease. He dreaded the thought of someone from his class confronting him, asking how he dared to continue struggling to meet the demand of the system. Didn't he know it was hopeless? Was he prepared to humiliate himself again, to have his ego shattered by intellectual rejection?

As he made his way to the library to look up the case, he was almost ashamed that he had felt so self-conscious about wanting to write on to law review. There had been an overwhelming air of resentment and self-pity among many of those who had survived the first year of law school but who had not reached the pinnacle of success, but there was no reason for him or any of his classmates to feel insecure about themselves or their intellect. If he were to give up and forget about at least trying to write on to law review, he would lapse into the same type of bitterness gripping his colleagues, allowing himself to be victimized by the indoctrination process.

He sat down in the main part of the library to read the Iranian hostage case, poring over the language of the opinion carefully to spot the issues and identify some major holding. The opinion itself was not extraordinary, although the facts of the case certainly were. He followed Marilyn's advice and read the concurrence of one of the justices, which shed little light on any issues on which he could focus for this paper.

Earl realized that he had a large research project ahead of him into the area of international law and presidential powers that would have to be completed before he could even begin to write his paper, due in three weeks. He looked up at the clock on the wall. The library would close in an hour. He would have to start his research another time. Besides, he wanted to get home early for a good night's sleep.

He had an arraignment the next morning on his beer case.

The next day, Earl felt curiously calm as he entered the packed courtroom for his arraignment. The long drive on his motorcycle in the morning had relaxed him. As he sat near the back he surveyed the assemblage. Most of the people there were young men. He overheard the people in front of him talking about how the city had decided to crack down on the youths who invaded their small coastal city from the university. Businesses favored the influx, but many locals apparently felt that these frolicking young people were an undesirable element.

When the judge came to the bench and announced that each had been assessed a $50 fine, which they could pay and then leave, many people in the audience began searching through their pockets and purses to scrape up the amount requested. The judge then began to call each defendant's name. As each of the hapless students approached the bench, Earl watched impassively, thinking about his research and the bygone era he had explored in his imagination. But this was real, even though there was a sort of carnival atmosphere to the whole affair. People looked at each other timidly, shuffling to the front of the room reluctantly. Some said, "guilty with an excuse" or tried to take some other clever middle ground with the judge.

When his name was finally called, Earl approached the bench and was asked how he pled. "Not guilty."

"Do you have the funds to hire a lawyer?"

"No, sir."

"I'll appoint the public defender. Please step over there."

He was led over to a small group of people sitting to the side in the jury box, some of whom looked like they had seen more than their fair share of jail cells and courtrooms. The one sitting next to him, a washed-out looking man with stringy hair, leaned over and whispered to him.

"What are you charged with?"

"Possession," Earl said with an air of gravity, then in a conspiratorial whisper, "of beer."

The man with stringy hair looked at him, puzzled. A few minutes later, a young man in a shabby suit walked towards the defendants assembled in the jury box, sifting through a stack of files. He whispered to each briefly before moving to the next defendant. When he stood in front of Earl, he was looking at his files, glancing up at him.

"Let's see now, you must be –"

"Earl Warren."

"Yeah, right. Very funny. I suppose this alleged drug addict next to you is William O. Douglas, right? Or is he the president of the United States?"

"No, my name is really Earl Warren. My parents never read the newspapers, so they didn't realize that they were condemning me to a lifetime of stupid jokes when they named me."

"Sonofabitch." The young man had found Earl's file. He looked at Earl as if seeing him for the first time. "You are Earl Warren. What is a titan of actual legal thinking doing in a courtroom such as this?"

"You must be the public defender."

"I'm Sid White. Here's my card." He thrust the card in Earl's hand. "I'll have to talk to you later about your case."

"Can I leave now?"

"Sure, sure. Just make sure you're here for trial. I'll give you the trial date later. I'll call you to discuss your case more, okay?"

He walked over to another defendant, looking through a stack of files in his hands as he spoke. He was obviously preoccupied with a number of other more pressing cases. Earl nodded to the man with the stringy hair and made his way out of the courtroom.

That night in the smoking room, Earl sat busily reading over cases and jotting down notes under Marilyn's watchful eye. He knew she assumed he was working on his paper, when in actuality most of the cases he was reading were from the prohibition era which had little to do with international law. He was not trying to deceive her, but he welcomed the chance to concentrate on the task at hand without being distracted by a debate with her on the relative importance of his law review paper to the brief he was writing on the constitutionality of his beer citation.

Within a week he began drafting his brief, carefully weaving his painstaking research into the circumstances of his case. He spent days just on the section of the brief describing the facts, putting the case in the best possible light without distortion. He read and revised his arguments and analysis several times and checked his citations again for accuracy. After proofreading his handwritten brief for the last time, he hired a typist and waited anxiously for the finished product.

The next day he went back to the smoking room. He had not been there for several days. "Look what the cat dragged in," Mark said as Earl walked through the door with an armload of books. "Been working on your masterpiece of international law?"

"Actually, I'm just now getting started," he said as he let the books down on the table with a loud thud.

"You better hurry. You only have a week left to become the next John Foster Dulles."

"I know. Don't tell Marilyn, but I've been working on a secret project the past couple days."

"Speak of the devil."

Marilyn had just walked into the room. She looked at the pile of books on the table in front of Earl.

"I hope you don't have a lot of research to do, Earl. By now you should have already completed your first draft, you know."

Earl just smiled at her weakly and looked at Mark, who gave him a smirk and then buried his head back in his books.

"This is a hard topic, Marilyn. There are very few cases in the area of international law and foreign relations. A lot of this paper will have to be based on articles and books written by international law scholars. Maybe I chose a bad topic."

Marilyn just looked at him, expressionless.

With a shrug, he sat down to begin reading over some of the cases and authorities he had collected. He felt drained after writing his beer brief and was still preoccupied with thoughts of prohibition. He was having doubts about how well he would do on this paper with so little time before the deadline. But at least he had chosen a topic that would hold his interest.

After a few hours of reading, he realized why there were so few court cases in the area of foreign relations. The courts in prior cases deferred to Congress and particularly the president in foreign affairs. The Supreme Court had even devised a theory of law whereby the powers associated with foreign affairs, which at colonial times had resided with the King of England, had been transferred to the president as the most closely analogous unit of the new American government.

This theory of law was based on an article written by George Sutherland, who later became the Supreme Court Justice who wrote this theory into law.

For practical reasons which cannot be denied, the courts and Congress have given broad powers to the president during times of international crisis such as the seizure of Americans in Tehran. But this almost total lack of oversight by these two branches of government over the third creates a large loophole in the careful system of checks and balances envisioned by the founders of the Constitution. In addition to the potential for the exercise of enormous, unchecked powers by the president, the abdication of the traditional roles of Congress and the judiciary in the American system of government has left the president and the other nations of the world with little authoritative legal precedent through court decisions or statutes from Congress that defines even the most basic principles of international law.

In the case of the Iranian hostages, the president made a deal with Tehran whereby the hostages were released in exchange for the transfer of billions of dollars of assets frozen in the United States. The first installment of the "ransom" was paid immediately upon the release of the hostages, which took place on his last day as president. The second (and largest) part of the ransom was to be paid six months later. Several companies who had claims to the assets being transferred to Iran for the sale of military and other goods and services to the Shah sued the incoming administration of the newly-elected successor president to block the transfer.

Although apparently troubled by the vast power of the president in wiping out billions of dollars worth of claims made by private companies (otherwise the justices wouldn't have written an opinion at all), the Supreme Court allowed the transfer without scrutinizing the transaction made by the president. The Court simply deferred to this exercise of power by the executive branch, to which Congress had also acquiesced, as a necessary arrow in the president's quiver during negotiations with other governments in times of crisis.

When he first read the case, Earl agreed that the Supreme Court obviously could not undercut the president by negating a deal for the release of the hostages. Future presidents would have difficulty negotiating with foreign governments if they could not deliver on their promises. That is probably why the Supreme Court has stayed out of international law.

But then he began to wonder if the result would really be so devastating. The president, in the midst of negotiations with a hostile power, would not be able to make a promise that was unfair or illegal under international law because he could not deliver. Why should the president be allowed to make such a deal anyway? Besides which, a president in a similar situation could explain to his adversary that the independent court system of his country would likely not approve of such a deal. This would add an additional element to these types of negotiations that would induce both the president and foreign powers to give due regard to international law but would not deprive the president of the power to make a deal under terms fair to everyone concerned, including private individuals and companies.

Within two days Earl had the basic outlines of his paper. But he had much to do and little time within which to do it. He was just beginning to type the first lines when the typist called.

His brief was finished.

The next day Earl picked up his brief on the way to the law school. He was in the lobby of the library making copies when Marilyn walked up to him.

"A first draft of your paper?" she asked, peering over his shoulder. Startled, Earl quickly slammed the cover of the copy machine over his brief and turned around, blocking her view.

"Uh, not exactly. Are you headed for the smoking room?"

She nodded.

"I'll meet you there in a minute. I'm almost done. I want to show you something."

She looked at him with a curious expression, and then a smile. "Okay," she said before heading back into the library towards the smoking room.

When he walked into the smoking room, he spotted Marilyn at the table and sat down next to her.

"This is what I have been working on the past couple of days," he whispered to her as he slipped a copy of the brief in front of her on the table. "Excuse me, I have to get back to work on my law review paper." He left as she looked down at the brief and started turning the pages.

Earl found himself too distracted to think about his paper. He went outside to an empty bench and sat down to read his newly-typed brief. Words scrawled on a page by hand are almost unrecognizable when transformed into the majesty of the printed word. He read the brief once quickly, looking for typographical errors. Then he read it again, trying to imagine himself as some objective person (like a judge) reading this material for the first time. He wondered how the judge assigned to his case would react, or if he would read the brief at all.

Then he saw Marilyn walking towards him. She sat down at the bench, handing him her copy of the brief and looking at him with a mixture of disapproval and amusement.

"So this is what you have been working on?"

"What do you think?"

"I think you won't make law review, but you wrote one hell of a brief on the right to drink beer."

"You know there is more to this than that. You were there. You know the feeling of having a police officer come down on you for such a trivial thing. The point is not the right to have a beer without being hassled by the police, the point is one of individual freedom. What have we come to in this country when we can't even enjoy the simple pleasures of life without having some fucking cop breathing down your neck?"

"I know, Earl. I was pretty upset, too, at the time. But you can't fight every injustice. You have to look at what is most important. Right now the most important thing is your legal career. Making law review is far more important than vindicating your rights in this case."

"Oh yeah? What do you think the bar association will think about this little criminal conviction if I don't fight this? Do you think they will have the same attitude? Just pay the two dollars, and we'll forget your criminal record?"

Marilyn gave him a look of consternation. He was following his instincts in reacting to this beer incident, but he knew that Marilyn was thinking of these more sinister ramifications. So was he. She reached out and stroked his face, giving him a sort of "what-am-I-going-to-do-with-you" expression. He took her hand and pulled her towards him.

"Don't worry. I have a brilliant concept for this law review paper. I'll be done in a few days."

"You'll have to. It's due Friday."

That Friday he slipped the paper he had typed himself into the mailbox of the law review.

Back in the smoking room, he sat down to read the paper again, exhausted.

Despite the time constraints he had pieced together what he thought was a respectable historical account of how the judicial and legislative branches of government had ceded limitless power to the chief executive during so-called "national emergencies" and foreign affairs. In his paper Earl objected to the "ransom" agreement entered into with Tehran by the president, and approved by his successor, at the expense of the rights of American claimants. Such a course of action would surely only encourage the taking of more hostages.

Besides, giving the president power to barter away the claims of these companies gave businesses less assurances that obligations incurred in the course of international transactions would be enforced in accordance with international law, thereby adversely affecting international trade. As a matter of policy, neither the courts nor the executive branch, should approve of agreements that rewarded illegal acts of terrorism by paying ransom, especially when the rights of others and the need for some semblance of international order were forfeited in the bargain.

As he read his paper in the smoking room, Earl was not aware of newspaper reports indicating that campaign workers for the man who later was elected president, concerned about rumors that the sitting president was about to make a deal for the release of the hostages, made contact with the Iranians to ensure that no deal was made that might affect the outcome of the election. Years later, in an attempt to obtain the release of more hostages seized by groups supported by Iran, the new president's administration again paid what was, in effect, ransom, creating a major scandal for the presidency.

Earl looked over his paper one last time. His theories may prove to be controversial. The president was very popular, and he wasn't sure how political law review was. His paper was also not nearly as neatly typed as his beer brief. He began to wonder if he had subconsciously sabotaged his paper by focusing too much attention on his beer brief. Maybe Marilyn was right. Maybe he had gotten too carried away with this beer thing and should have spent more time on his paper.

A week later he was sitting in the smoking room, actually reading his textbook on international law. He had decided to concentrate as much of his remaining studies as he could to international law and related topics and had found the subject as interesting as constitutional law.

Marilyn came into the smoking room with a grim expression on her face. She slipped into a chair next to Earl and said nothing for a while.

"I didn't make it, did I?" Earl finally whispered.

"I'm sorry, Earl. I read your paper and thought it was pretty good. I think the topic was just too obscure. Actually, some of the editors just didn't understand what you were talking about. And, to be honest, your footnotes could have used a little more meat to them."

"I told you there was not a lot of case law in this area."

"At least you tried, Earl. A lot of people in your class didn't even bother to try to write on. I'm proud of you."

She reached her arm over his shoulders and squeezed. For some reason her contact unleashed a wave of emotion from deep inside of him. He turned his head slightly so that she could not see he was fighting back tears. He was surprised at his own reaction. He wasn't sure if he was experiencing a release of the strain under which he had been placed or deep sorrow.

"I guess I should have spent more time on this paper and less time on that damn beer brief," he said after a minute, when he had regained his composure.

She rubbed his shoulder and smiled broadly. "Earl, that's just the type of person you are. You can't help it. When you feel wronged, you fight back. To tell you the truth, I think I'd rather have the Earl who stands on principle than the one who sits up late at night reading boring law review articles."

"Really?" She was trying to make him feel better and was having some success, if only because she was standing by him.

"Really," she said before giving him a quick kiss, another smile, and abruptly getting up to leave.

Later that afternoon Earl was at home, staring out the window. He was thinking more about Marilyn than about his ill-fated hostage paper. The phone interrupted his thoughts. "Hello?"

"Mr. Chief Justice? This is your lawyer, Sid White."

"Sid. How did you like my brief?"

"Your brief was fucking great. I filed it with the court, and we had a hearing today. Guess what happened?"

"Ten years hard labor?"

"The charges were dropped. The state told the judge that they had to drop the charges because the cop had you dispose of the only physical evidence – the two bottles of beer – which is a load of crap since they could have had the cop testify, plus you admitted in your brief that you had the beer."

"Then why did they drop the charges?"

"Someone in the prosecutor's office told me that when they got your brief, they panicked. The city was afraid that if the law was declared unconstitutional, they would not be able to collect fines from all these college kids. So they decided to get rid of your case."

"You mean they're going to keep citing these kids even though they know the law is unconstitutional? That's not right, Sid. Can't we get an injunction or, or *something*?"

"Hey, Earl, what are you upset about? You won. You should be happy. You can't right every injustice, you know?"

"Yeah, I know. Thanks Sid."

CHAPTER VI
ROAD TO RUIN

Earl walked into the pub, waiting momentarily as his eyes adjusted to the darkness. He saw Frank waving to him from a booth near the rear of the pub. He waved back and proceeded back towards the booth, his eyes slowly adjusting to the drastic change in light from the bright summer day to the dank interior of his surroundings. When he reached the booth, he slid into a seat, nodding at Frank and murmuring greetings to the others gathered at the booth.

"Is this the meeting of the cell?" Earl asked after a short period of uncomfortable silence.

The two people sitting with Frank looked at him momentarily with alarm, but soon relaxed their expression as he gave Earl a ready smile and a slight nod.

"Yes, comrade," he said.

"Well then, perhaps we should discuss the revolution. What do you have to report, comrade?"

"Cut the shit, Earl. This is Ralph and Mark, two dedicated members of our new political party, 'Solidarity,' named after the democratic movement in Poland back in the good old days."

Earl nodded at both of them briefly. "So what is the status of the election?" he asked, turning to Frank.

"Thanks to the research you provided, Earl, we were able to get most of what we wanted as far as campaigning on campus. The people in student government were intimidated enough to allow us to campaign among the students. We are trying to work on themes that are attractive to the student body"

"Well, what did you come up with?"

Frank paused, looking at his compatriots for approval.

"Well, the consensus is that we push for a progressive radio station. You know, the station on campus has turned into a completely commercial pop station with very little new music and no jazz. We'd like to see a little more variety, maybe some reggae or even rap music on the station."

"That is certainly an issue of burning social consequence," said Earl, sipping his beer.

"Ah, but what you do not realize is that the station on campus is run through the university's journalism department. This proposed station would be run by student government.

The administration would not be able to censor any of our broadcasts. We would be free to criticize administration decisions and discuss issues free from control by the university, broadcasting to thousands of students on campus and the general public."

"You mean, what on the surface appears to be an issue totally lacking in substance and redeeming social value that appeals to the musical taste of the students is in reality a plot to install a major propaganda apparatus for the revolution?"

"Precisely," Frank replied as his two friends gave a startled expression. "We also have a few more issues. One is to make the university use money collected from the investment of student funds for loans to needy students. Ralph here has discovered that the university has such an account, but we haven't quite figured out what this money is being used for. Rumor has it that the money is being funneled somehow to student government types who do favors for the administration. Anyway, I found a statute that allows this money to be used for student loans. With the budget cutbacks to financial aid, a lot of students need another source of money for tuition and books."

"Frank, I support everything you're saying, but what makes you think student government is going to go for this after the election, especially if what you suspect is true?"

"That's the point, Earl. These ideas are being presented as referendums for the students to vote on directly. If they pass, student government has to go along. Students will not have to rely on promises of candidates, so we think they will come out to vote in greater numbers. Hopefully, Solidarity will ride the coattails on these issues into office. Which brings me to why I asked you here, Earl. We need a candidate from the law school. We want you to be our candidate."

Earl froze for a moment, his glass of beer suspended in his hand inches from his lips, which remained protruded for a few seconds as he looked at Frank, his two friends, and then back at Frank. His two friends sat expressionless.

"Thanks, but no thanks, Frank."

"Come on, Earl, I know you believe in what we are doing. You'd make a perfect politician. You're bright, personable, and you have great name recognition at the law school."

"I'm sorry, Frank, and I'm flattered that you asked. I believe in what you're trying to do, but I don't believe in the system. I'm way too cynical about the political process in general and student government in particular. I couldn't become part of something that I don't agree with. Besides, I'm not cut out to be a politician. I'm basically a loner. An outsider. An outcast. My way of thinking is too far outside the mainstream, and I'm too honest to try and disguise my feelings or schmooze people I can't stand so I can get a favor. I'm not saying every person involved in politics is bad, and I'm not saying that I am above it all. I am what I am, and I'm not a politician."

Frank's friends Mark and Ralph did not seem to be too crestfallen as Earl made this announcement. In fact, they seemed almost relieved. Frank didn't miss a beat.

"Okay, Earl. But we need someone from the law school to run, and you were our only candidate."

"You mean, I was the first choice on a list of one?"

Mark and Ralph, the two Solidarity officials, couldn't help but smile at that last comment.

Frank just shrugged.

"I have an idea, Frank," Earl finally said. "I think I can con Marilyn into doing it for you."

"Marilyn Hollander? From law review? That would be great. How would you get her to do it?"

"I'll appeal to her social consciousness, her sense of manifest destiny, her innate skills, and the need for leadership on behalf of all the law students." Earl paused for effect, taking a sip of his beer. "Then I'll tell her it will look good on her resume when she's job hunting after graduation.

She'll do it. Besides," he added with a sly grin, "she'll do anything for me."

Frank just looked at him and smiled. "Oh, that reminds me. I have to recruit volunteers to assist me in going to the sorority houses to convince them to back our proposal to add an equal rights amendment to the student government constitution. Would you like to go, or would Marilyn object?"

Frank's face broke into a broad grin after his last comment. Marilyn was a hot property at the law school, and he knew that she was not taken, although she and Earl were close.

"Why, Frank, I didn't know you were so involved in women's issues, except on a personal level, of course."

"Are you suggesting that I attend feminist rallies just on the off chance that someone may inspire spontaneous bra-burning, giving me some sort of cheap thrill?"

"No, but I'm sure that if that happened, you would suggest a spontaneous wet T-shirt contest. Purely as a fundraiser for the cause, of course."

They both snickered. Then Frank sat back in his chair.

"Isn't this male bonding stuff great?" he said, as he slapped Ralph on the back. Ralph's eyes got big as he looked at Frank with a curious expression. Earl laughed.

The next day Earl stopped Marilyn in the hall to ask if she wanted to run. She looked at him as if he were crazy.

"We can talk about it on our ride to Miami," Earl said. They were leaving together at the end of the week for the Fourth of July holidays. She wanted to visit her parents. He was going to a wedding of an old college roommate.

Early that Friday morning Earl pulled out into the street and headed for the interstate.

Marilyn was still a little groggy. As they approached the ramp, he looked over at her.

"So, are you going to work on your total tan now?" He looked over at her with a grin. She just managed to give him a glare through her drooping eyelids. "Maybe we should stop for some coffee."

"None for me," she muttered.

After getting his "jumbo" coffee at the convenience store near the ramp, Earl pulled into the traffic on the interstate, balancing the huge Styrofoam cup between his legs. He eased up to a respectable speed to blend in with the other cars flying down the highway before carefully removing the lid on his coffee, his eyes darting back and forth from the steaming cup to the road. He took a sip and winced, partly in reaction to the hot liquid touching his lips, but mostly because of the strong hard taste of convenience store coffee.

He glanced around at the other cars on the highway. Many of the cars still had headlights on even though the sun had risen over an hour earlier. Earl's mind wandered back to times that he had had to drive through the night. He looked through the windows of these lost souls as they passed by, trying to imagine what urgent cause led them to such a lonely trek.

His thoughts made him think of their own long journey. The drive to Miami was a grueling seven-hour trip past landscape that varied very little. After the rows of pine trees on this first leg of the trip, they would see mostly nondescript vegetation and farmland, passing an occasional cluster of gas stations, hotels, and the trustworthy convenience stores nestled near the exit ramps to the interstate.

Earl settled back in his seat, the coffee warming the inside of his body. A few beads of sweat formed on his brow which he wiped with his hand. He tilted the vent upwards until he felt the artificial breeze of the air conditioning blowing on his face.

Thoughts about the length of the drive were purposefully driven from his mind in a familiar way he often used on these long journeys. He allowed his mind to run free, dwelling on subjects from current events to the human condition. From time to time he would pause in his thoughts, looking out to some spot along the highway. He saw a large shade tree and a path that disappeared into the trees and brush. He pictured that scene in his mind's eye, drawing the tree closer as if by a zoom lens on a camera. He thought about minutes passing as the scene remained the same. Hours and then days would pass under the tree. Maybe a small boy or a group of children would play under the tree, or just talk about unimportant things, the experience of such simple events in their lives etched forever in their memories. The tree and bushes stood silently by, days and then years passing. A hundred years may have passed, changes in the scene taking shape too slowly for the children or a passerby to notice.

Time and nature ran their course steadily. This inspired awe in Earl, whose experience under the tree was from a distance and lasted but a split second of time. His imagination had to carry him to that spot and through the years in an instant and with a mere glance.

Then further down the road, he would see a dilapidated tin shack and wonder of the lives spent at that scene and the silent march of time. There were so many scenes, so many lives and experiences that were so intimate to someone, but so alien to Earl. He was a voyeur for an instant. With each passing scene upon which he intruded from his vantage point, he thought of the sheer magnitude of life's experiences just in the short distances he had traveled, sampling here and there scenes from which he extrapolated a lifetime.

These thoughts consumed him almost in a trance as the hours in Marilyn's car were spent. They had been traveling for almost three hours, and Earl marked the point when they would soon reach halfway through their trip. Marilyn had slept most of the time, stirring once when he had passed through the toll onto the Florida Turnpike. Earl had put the car on cruise control, setting his speed at 55 miles per hour. Traffic had become a little heavier on the turnpike. He noticed a blue van approaching him quickly from behind and pulled into the right lane to let him pass.

The van screamed past by at least 75 miles per hour.

Soon Earl came upon a group of cars going very slowly. He looked down at his speedometer to check their speed and his own, puzzled for a moment. Then he glanced up at his rear-view mirror and was startled to see the grill of a car pressed up against his own. He hit the accelerator and looked for an opening in the right lane. At first he thought the car behind them was an emergency vehicle trying to pass. But when he glanced up again at his mirror, he saw the telltale flashing blue lights of the Florida Highway Patrol.

He pulled into the right lane and slowed the car, expecting the trooper to pass him. Instead, the trooper pulled behind him in the right lane. Earl realized for the first time that the trooper was pulling him over.

Marilyn by this time began to show a little life. "What's going on, Earl? What happened?"

"I don't know" was all he could say as he pulled to a stop on the side of the highway. "Were you speeding?"

"No. Marilyn, you better give me your registration and proof of insurance while I talk to this guy."

"Wait a second." She reached into the glove compartment and pulled out the papers, neatly stacked inside. "Here."

He took the papers and headed back to the trooper, who had just gotten out of his cruiser.

"Here's my license, registration, and proof of insurance," Earl said, handing the papers to the trooper. He knew the law and wanted to cooperate as much as he could. But he noticed that the trooper had already begun making out a ticket.

"Do you know how fast you were going, sir?"

"Fifty-five?" Earl replied with an earnest look.

"I clocked you at 74 miles per hour when you were slowing down, sir."

Earl was vaguely amused by the trooper, who was as young as he was, addressing him as "sir."

"I think there is some mistake here, Officer." He was trying to be even more polite than the trooper was. "May I take a look at your radar gun?"

Earl made his way around to the passenger side of the cruiser. Before the officer could say a word, he slipped into the seat, looking at the radar. The screen was blank.

"There's no reading, Trooper . . . Ogden." Earl read the trooper's name on the name tag on his breast. He was trying to be respectful and friendly.

"We don't do that here, sir" Trooper Ogden said. He was still making out the ticket as Earl got out of the cruiser.

"Look, Officer, if I were guilty, I would just own up to it and pay the fine. But you have made a mistake. I think maybe you clocked that blue van racing down the road like a bat outta hell that passed me a few miles back." Earl knew as he spoke that he was getting this ticket no matter what he said. Trooper Ogden kept writing as he was talking. When he finished writing, he tore the ticket off, handing the ticket and his papers to Earl.

"Sir, here is your ticket. You can go to court if you want to, but let me tell ya, in this county if you don't pay your ticket and go to court, it's for double or nothin'."

"What do you mean?"

"This here ticket is for $50."

"Fifty bucks?"

"That's right. If you go to court and lose, the judge will fine you twice as much. You just think about that before you decide to make a fuss about this here ticket. If you want my advice, you'd be better off just paying the fifty bucks, sir."

Earl walked back to the car in a daze. He slid in behind the wheel. Marilyn was looking at him expectantly.

"I got a $50 fine. And if I go to court, it'll be for double or nothing," he finally said. "What? I thought you said you weren't speeding?"

"I wasn't."

"Dammit, Earl. Do you know what this is going to do to my insurance premiums?"

"I'll take care of it, Marilyn." She glared at him for a moment. "I'm sorry. But I swear to God I wasn't speeding. I think he clocked that blue van that went racing by."

She settled back in her seat after a few seconds as he began to pull out into traffic. He winced slightly when he kicked up some dust and gravel as he took off.

Marilyn didn't notice.

CHAPTER VII
ROAD TAX

Earl peeked into the smoking room to see if Marilyn was inside. She was. He slipped inside and sat next to her, opening his textbook on International Economic Relations. Several weeks had passed since their return from the trip to Miami, and she had hardly mentioned his speeding ticket. He felt extremely guilty about the whole incident and wanted to find out if she was still angry with him. They both knew that a speeding ticket for a person driving a red Firebird would make her insurance skyrocket.

Lately, Marilyn was in a very good mood. She had even agreed to run as a Solidarity candidate with little hesitation. Earl was torn between ruining her good mood and broaching the subject of his speeding ticket during an opportune time when she may be more forgiving.

"I have my court hearing tomorrow," he finally said when the room was nearly deserted. "I thought you already won that beer thing," Mark interjected from a corner of the room, eager for a break from the monotony of his studies for final exams. "No, this is another case. I got a ticket for speeding."

"Damn, Earl, you'll be a seasoned trial lawyer before you even get out of law school at the rate you're going."

"It's not by choice, believe me."

"You can always just pay the fine and be done with it, Earl. You know what they say, 'you can't fight city hall.'"

"I know, I know. They also say, 'pay the two dollars.' But there is a little more at stake here than a two dollar fine."

"I see. A matter of principle."

Earl was actually thinking about Marilyn's insurance rates going up and what to him was a stiff $50 fine. He was very uncomfortable with the idea that he was in no position to reimburse Marilyn for her increase in insurance premiums – not to mention the fact that with this fine, he would probably have to forego the purchase of some books next semester.

"Why don't you use my car to get to court," said Marilyn. Earl was surprised. "Are you kidding?"

"No, I'm not. You'll be in the middle of red-neck country. You can't ride in there on your hog motorcycle, or they'll lock you up and throw away the key."

"Yeah, I can see the newspaper headlines," said Mark, framing an imaginary banner headline in the air with his hands. "Biker law student jailed for traffic offense. Classmates pass the hat to raise bail."

"Very funny, but I suppose you're right. Seems like cases are decided by something other than the truth – or the law."

"Come by tomorrow morning. I'll give you the keys. I'll get a ride into school from my roommate," Marilyn said.

"Are you sure?"

Marilyn looked into his eyes, giving him that warm smile that made him tingle all over his body. Mark suddenly became very engrossed in his books. "Sure, I'm sure."

Early the next morning Earl was still thinking about Marilyn as he merged into traffic on the interstate. She managed a weak smile through eyes that were little more than slits when she met him at her doorstep to give him her keys. Even in an over-sized T-shirt, hair snarled in disarray, she looked enticing.

He wasn't sure if she was humoring his passion for justice or if she thought he might get the judge to throw his ticket out. For Earl, fighting the ticket was almost a reflex action. He was not speeding and should not pay a fine.

He always believed that in a court of law, truth would somehow always be revealed. The rest would fall into place.

The same was true in traffic court – or at least it should be.

He had to juggle his map and the steering wheel to find the right exit to the state road leading to the small rural town where he was notified to appear in court. He followed the road past farmland and pastures enveloped in the early morning mist. Gradually, he began to pass old gas stations and austere strip stores, sure signs that he was approaching civilization. He was struck by the near poverty of the area that was typical of small rural towns in northern Florida.

Earl stopped at a railroad crossing, watching the train pass by with cars loaded with livestock, tractors, and unmarked cars with unknown cargoes. He was fumbling for his map to get his bearings as the last car passed when he stopped short, his gaze fixed on what lay before him.

Rising from the mist, past the cornfield to his left, was an imposing, and ominous-looking, three-story building that dwarfed anything and everything in sight, dominating the landscape. Earl was startled from his momentary trance by the old pickup honking from behind. The driver was yelling something about "Yankees" as Earl put the car in gear and headed down the road, the building growing larger and more menacing. As he got closer, he could see that the oval-shaped building had a sophisticated architectural style and had been just recently constructed.

"Buford County Courthouse," he read aloud from the front of the building. *Named after some prominent member of the community from the past, like a slave trader or something,* he thought to himself as he pulled into the parking lot.

He was awestruck by the building as he passed through the gleaming glass doors at the front entrance, a feeling that was probably intentionally considered in the design of the structure. Inside, the modern design continued as Earl entered a circular antechamber with windows behind which sat court clerks. He wandered forward towards one of the windows, his hearing notice clutched in his hand.

"May I hep ya?" asked the woman behind the window. The southern accent and hospitality was oddly out of place. Earl handed her his notice without speaking. She directed him down a hall to one of the traffic courtrooms.

At the time Earl didn't stop to think how such a poor rural county could finance such an audacious building. He was too busy adjusting to the culture shock and thinking about what he would say to the judge when his case was called. He walked into the courtroom and took his customary seat in the rear, studying the space-age bench and jury box, glistening railings, and brand new carpeting. He detected the subtle odor of newly constructed rooms that fades with time and human occupancy.

Court was called to order, Judge Clyde Akins presidin'. Earl sat and watched as the judge upheld every ticket handed out to the hapless motorists who protested their innocence. Earl noticed a pattern: As each person was found guilty, their fine was doubled, sometimes with court costs added. Finally, a defendant charged with running a red light fessed up, throwing himself upon the mercy of the court.

"That's what I like to hear, young feller. No need to take up the Court's time with tom foolery. Just step on out to the clerk and pay your fine."

Earl had spent some time researching at the law library. He found a number of cases where traffic judges had been reversed for penalizing motorists who pleaded innocent and asked to have their case heard by the judge. But Judge Akins wasn't stupid enough to announce his "double or nothin'" policy on the record. He let troopers and sheriffs spread the word. Spectators who watched cases go before them could see what was happening. Earl still couldn't believe it.

"Earl Warren," called the bailiff.

"Well now, I been dreamin' bout getten that meddlin' Yankee chief justice before me for a long time. You ain't related, are ya, son?"

"No, sir."

"Good. I wouldn't want to hafta recuse myself. Now, what is your story, Mister Warren?"

"I'm not guilty, Your Honor. I think maybe Trooper Ogden here clocked a blue van that went racing by me by mistake."

"Trooper Ogden, that so?"

"No sir. I read that red sports car a-goin' 74 miles per hour on the turnpike."

"Was your radar gun workin' right?"

"Yes, sir."

"Your Honor, I–"

The judge interrupted Earl with a raised hand. "I know some of ya'll in MY-ama don't believe in radar guns. I know Judge Nesbitt down there; he's a friend of mine. But in these parts we swear by em, boy." The reference was to a judge in Miami who threw out speeding tickets based on radar guns, citing studies that showed the devices clocking trees at 75 miles per hour and a house going 45. The controversy over radar guns and the judge drew national media attention.

"Judge, I will say Mr. Warren here had a good attitude," Ogden offered, looking over at Earl sympathetically. He knew he was about to get the gavel.

"I find you guilty. Fine is $100."

"But, Your Honor –"

"Look, son, I made my ruling."

"Your Honor, I'd like to make an objection for the record." Earl remembered from Stevens' class that any constitutional grounds for reversal had to be made at the earliest possible stage in the trial proceedings. But his case was decided so quickly he didn't have time to get a word in edgewise.

Judge Akins' eyes narrowed. "Where'd you say you worked?"

"I didn't. I'm a law student."

"What's your objection, Mr. Law Student?"

"I object based on the Fourteenth and Sixth Amendments to the United States Constitution, Your Honor."

The judge peered down at Earl, seething. "Did you say the Fourth Amendment, son?"

"No, Sixth, your honor."

"You ain't got no grounds under the Fourth, you know."

"I know that, Judge. That is why I said *Sixth*."

"Well, I'm glad they at least taught you somethin' in that law school. Pay your fine outside, *Counselor*," finished the judge with a wave of his hand, emphasizing the word "counselor" without disguising his contempt.

Earl walked out, numb. The whole experience was like a dream. He couldn't believe the attitude of the judge or that he had the guts to stand up to him. He walked over to the clerk to ask about his fine. They wanted his money right then. He didn't have a hundred dollars. He couldn't quite believe what the trooper had said about doubling his fine and had only brought $50 he had managed to scrape together. The clerk gave him 10 days to pay the fine. Earl signed some papers, his hands shaking noticeably. He walked across the antechamber and eased himself onto a bench, as if his body ached with pain.

He watched for a moment as people came out of the courtrooms and made their way to pay their fines. Some seemed to take the justice meted out in stride. Most had a look of bewilderment or anger. They gathered in lines that formed at the windows of the clerks, shuffling forward sheepishly like lost souls trapped in a common nightmare. Earl tried to imagine what outrage had been perpetrated against each by the judge, leaving them feeling as cheated and helpless as he felt.

He had had enough courtroom experiences by this time to dispel the exalted vision of courts, judges and justice. But he was not so cynical as to imagine that a judge would forego all pretense at fairness and impartiality, resentful that a person who appeared before him would question his judgment. Looking around the spacious antechamber, and up the domed cathedral ceiling, he suddenly realized that this was all part of a more sophisticated version of the typical rural speed trap. The court hearings were a sham at best. At worst, they were a means to enhance the revenue collected from motorists by distributing a "surtax" to those who asked to have their cases heard.

The shock and frustration Earl originally felt began to give way to feelings of righteous indignation. The courts of this country, even traffic courts, were not a front for the collection of a road tax in the guise of speeding tickets. Neither were they like a rigged poker game where people who appeared before the judge gambled for "double or nothing" and always lost. As he sat there on the bench, he knew that none of the people lining up to make their contribution to the monument to the perversion of justice in which they had all assembled would fight any further.

That was the beauty of the system. Contesting a relatively small fine would cost more than the fine itself. Besides which, a person who would make a big deal out of such a minor problem would be dismissed as a crackpot. Judge Akins knew what he was doing was illegal, and more importantly morally wrong, but he also knew no one would ever challenge his actions.

Earl found himself walking directly towards the windows. He noticed the young woman who had given him his papers sitting behind a sign that said "NEXT WINDOW PLEASE." She gave him a friendly look that seemed to say, "I know, I'm sorry you were railroaded."

He walked towards her. "I'm closed."

"I know, darlin'," Earl said, managing his best southern drawl. "I just want to ask you a question."

"What?"

"I didn't notice: Is there a court reporter in these here hearings with the judges?"

"Nope. But they do tape-record the hearings."

"How would I go about gettin' a tape of the hearing I had this mornin'?"

She hesitated a moment, looking around as if she didn't want to get caught. Then she gave Earl one of those looks, as if to say, *anything for you, sugar* and asked, "Why don't you give me your address and phone number, and I'll send you a copy?"

"I'd appreciate that. My name is–"

"Earl Warren, I know. And I have your case number, too." She looked at Earl and smiled again. He felt a little awkward but smiled back as he wrote down his address and number.

"Thank you very much."

"Any time," she replied, with an expression that left doubt as to exactly what he could thank her for at any time.

On his way out he asked someone else where the clerk who handles appeals was located. He was directed down a side hallway to an obscure office door with a small, handwritten sign taped to the door that said "Appeals." Inside he asked for forms to file an appeal and to waive the filing fees. The older man behind the counter eyed him suspiciously.

"What do you want those for?"

"Does that make a difference?"

After looking him over a few more seconds, the man gave him the forms. Earl was glad to finally get out of that building.

Later that afternoon, Earl described his experience in Buford County Court to a small audience in the smoking room. Marilyn listened without comment as he told his tale, with an occasional joke or observation offered by Mark.

"What's your next step? Burning Judge Akins in effigy?" Mark asked when Earl had finished.

"Are you crazy? If they don't have a Sixth Amendment in Buford, you think they would have a First Amendment? No, my next step is to file an appeal."

Mark let out a quiet laugh. The others just sort of shook their heads in disbelief and went back to their studies. Marilyn studied Earl for a few minutes in silence.

"I'm sorry, Marilyn. I'm making light of what happened, but I was really pretty shook up. Now I'm pissed off. If I had a fair hearing and lost, that would be different. I could accept that, pay the fine, and move on. But this is outrageous."

"You're right. And I've learned by now that you are who you are. I'd be disappointed if you didn't react this way. That's why I like you so much," she said, putting her arm around him as they walked out of the smoking room.

Earl put his around her, too, as they walked. Then in a whisper he said, "Besides which, when I file my appeal, I will get a stay of the fine, and your insurance rates won't go up." They looked at each other stand laughed.

A collective "SHHHHHH" came from the rows of students sitting at the tables. They snuck out of the library on their tiptoes, mouthing apologies.

CHAPTER VIII
FIRST MONDAY IN OCTOBER

By mid-October the summer session, and summer doldrums, were already a faded memory. Earl had filed his notice of appeal and motion to waive the appeal filing fee in the Buford County Court. His motion was granted, and the appeal was docketed in the circuit court. He also received an order in the mail granting his motion to stay the fine pending the appeal – signed by Judge Akins.

When he received the stay, Earl was encouraged. He began to feel that maybe the system was not so bad after all. Mistakes or injustices could be corrected in due course if the right levers were pulled and the right buttons pushed. He felt a reassuring sense of being more in control. He also had a vague feeling of power.

Getting to this point took some doing. Earl had spent hours reading and re-reading the confusing array of statutes and rules that apply to filing an appeal. His legal education had not prepared him for the mechanics of practicing law. Two semesters of civil procedure were required at the law school, and he had also taken a course of appellate procedure with Judge Whittaker.

But when the time came to draft a motion and figure out where to file a notice of appeal, he discovered that the most reliable authority was the clerk's office. He spoke at length with Mary Beth, the clerk who sent him the tape. She was very helpful.

He was still thinking about the vast difference between law school and the "real world" on his way to class when he spotted Frank sitting at one of the benches, reading the school newspaper. Every one of the student initiatives had been approved by the student body in the elections. But the coattails failed to materialize. Marilyn was the only Solidarity candidate to win a seat in the student senate, and she just barely beat out her opponent, whose platform consisted of a promise to have a keg party every Friday afternoon if elected. Earl had already started to lobby her to establish an international law review.

"Comrade! How goes the revolution?"

"Oh, hi, Earl," Frank replied, looking up from his paper.

"You know, I can't understand how Solidarity did so poorly when the voters liked all of our issues."

"Someone told me that the students didn't vote for us because they thought Solidarity meant we were communists," Frank said with a shrug.

Earl looked at him in disbelief. "How can they say that? Correct me if I'm wrong, but wasn't Solidarity the name of the labor movement in Poland that eventually overthrew the Communist government in power there?"

"Search me."

"So much for higher education in the fields of world history and civics."

Frank put down his paper and looked at Earl earnestly. "Yeah, but guess what?"

"What?"

"The president of student government just requisitioned the money for the radio station. He said that the vote by the students under the constitution of student government had the force of legislation. I already checked with the FCC, and the way is clear to set up the station. They can start to broadcast probably sometime next semester."

"All right!" Earl exclaimed as he grabbed Frank's arm. They grinned at each other in glee. Earl even felt his eyes start to glisten before he regained control. "I really expected SG to find some way to screw that up. I can't believe it."

"Yeah, well, Mark and Ralph still have their hands in SG. Mark was just made the SG auditor, as a matter of fact. He's an accounting major, you know."

"No, I didn't know. Well, that's fucking great, Frank. Maybe students will have a little more faith that their votes can make a difference. That makes it worth it."

"Yeah."

They both gathered up their books and started heading for class. Earl took in the subtle fragrances and cool air of the Florida autumn as he walked. He was in his final year of law school and was more than a little fatigued. He had attended school without taking a break as most other students had so that he could graduate early. With the full load of classes this term and in the winter, he would graduate after slightly more than two years of study, accomplishing what normally took at least three years. Then he could get on with his life.

He knew that in a few years, he would look back on his years in college and law school with fondness. Fall was a season in particular that he cherished. But soon he would end this chapter in his life and fulfill his childhood dream of becoming a lawyer.

At that same moment in time, in Washington, D.C., the coming of the fall season brought a different sort of atmosphere at the Supreme Court building. The term had begun, as was the custom, on the first Monday of October. The nine justices of the Court had resumed their busy schedules of conferences, oral arguments, and review of cert summaries and briefs after the summer recess.

In his spacious, ornate chambers, Chief Justice Moorehead was taking a late lunch. To the side of his huge mahogany desk was a large silver tray upon which sat the elegant china and silverware which had borne his repast. He sipped his tea, the small finger of his hand gracefully extended, as he looked over the notes of the speech he was to deliver that afternoon at a conference of law school deans and administrators.

Moorehead had fine features set into a plump face that was well-complemented by a shining white mane of hair that had long since turned gray. His large frame and even larger midsection cut an imposing figure whenever he entered a room. At 69 he had reached the twilight, and pinnacle, of his career, presiding as a justice "first among equals" on the highest court in the land. He felt deserving of all of the trappings of power and prestige – and, yes, even regal splendor – that his high office commanded.

"Pardon me, Chief," came the voice of his longtime secretary, Rosemary Woodward, over the intercom.

"What is it?" he asked tersely in his loud, baritone voice, daintily dabbing a white napkin on his mouth. He made no effort to disguise his annoyance at the interruption.

"It's Mr. Justice Wade on the line. Shall I tell him you're not available?"

"No, I'll take it . . . Hello, Harry?" Moorehead's tone had suddenly grown friendly.

"Hello, Chief. Hope I'm not interrupting anything," came the voice of Justice Wade on the line.

"Not at all."

"I just wanted to let you know that I was still working on that busing opinion. I know you're anxious to get a first draft, but it may take another week or two for some fine-tuning. I don't want to lose votes on this by writing a poorly-reasoned opinion."

"Just do the best you can, Harry. That's all I can ask."

After a few pleasantries, Moorehead put the phone back on the hook. "Spineless, utterly spineless." He looked up at the servant wearing a white jacket, towel draped over his arm, who had entered the room to clear the dishes as he made this comment about his colleague. He eyed the servant suspiciously. The servant went about his work without even noticing the hostile gaze fixed upon him by the chief.

Ever since that damnable book about the inner workings of the Supreme Court, Moorehead had become nearly obsessed with "security." He had admonished his own staff about leaks to the press and had even lectured the other justices about talking to reporters. The cloak of secrecy that surrounded the Supreme Court had to be maintained at all costs, and the chief justice had the duty to keep a tight control over any information that may be disseminated to the outside world.

The book had revealed embarrassing details of Moorehead's pomposity and his rank political manipulation of the decisions handed down by the high Court. The busing opinion about which Justice Wade had called was a case in point.

The justices met on a regular basis to vote on the outcome of cases brought before the Court. After each justice would cast their votes, the justice with the most seniority in the majority would decide which of the justices would write the opinion for that majority. If the chief justice was in the majority, he (or she) was entitled to designate who would write the opinion. The same rule applied to justices who made up the minority. The chief, or the senior justice if the chief was in the majority, had the right to designate the justice in the minority to write the dissenting opinion.

For years the justices followed this unwritten rule without incident.

When Moorehead took the throne, he realized that the course of future decisions, and the shape of constitutional law, could be influenced in accordance with the wording of an opinion. He decided that he would use his status as chief to choose authors of opinions in important cases that would word their opinions in such a way as to give the most restrictive interpretation to the rights of individuals and that would otherwise best reflect his own conservative philosophies. Toward that end, he began to "pass" when his turn to vote came – a practice that at first startled, and then annoyed the other justices. By the end of the vote, he would know what the outcome would be, and sometimes could even decide the outcome himself.

In the busing case, the vote was 5-3 to uphold the decision of the trial judge who had ordered massive busing of minority students to rectify the unequal funding between white schools and those relegated to minority areas. Moorehead, of course, was opposed to busing, which normally took the form of arguing that the state and local governments should decide the issue, complaining that "activist" federal judges were meddling in the proper exercise of power by the government. But in the busing case, he voted to uphold the judge, even though he wanted to reverse the case. This put him in the law books as favoring busing even though he was adamantly opposed to the whole idea, but more importantly, gave him the right to assign the opinion since he was now in the majority.

Moorehead assigned Wade to write the opinion because, of the five justices who had voted to affirm, he was the most conservative. Giving him the opinion meant that the wording would be the most restrictive and would deprive his nemesis, the legendary liberal Justice Baker, the right to write an opinion giving sweeping powers to judges trying to rectify race discrimination in the public schools. Because of his stature and the many years he had spent on the Supreme Court, Baker was the only justice that the chief thought could undermine his authority.

But Moorehead took comfort in the knowledge that, in time, the conservative philosophies he held would vanquish the shopworn theories of individual liberties and over-regulation of industry that Baker espoused. A succession of conservative presidents and the inability of the forces of liberalism to hold sway over the populace, much less elect a president, ensured that as the liberal justices grew old and then retired, the dwindling number of liberal justices would be overtaken by young, conservative justices who would wipe out the years of liberal dominance of the Supreme Court, replacing their outmoded ideas with a view of the constitution that gave fewer rights to individuals, particularly criminals, and more power to the government, especially the police, except when businesses were adversely affected by the unnecessary regulations born of New Deal liberalism.

Moorehead was not concerned with such things as a historical foundation for his conservative philosophies, or an analysis of the policies or effects of conservatism in general, or even as applied to an individual case. He left those details to the younger, more scholarly justices and his law clerks, who wrote his opinions for him. He only knew what he believed and that what he believed was right. The Supreme Court was nothing more than another battleground between the competing political forces of conservatism and liberalism.

He was determined that his side would be the ultimate winner.

The chief placed his speech into his breast pocket and leaned back in his chair for a moment, surveying his collection of antiques and framed photographs showing him swearing in the president and cavorting with assorted dignitaries. He had a feeling of deep satisfaction, and of destiny.

He felt power.

Outside the Supreme Court building he ducked down and into his waiting limousine. A group of young people in blue jeans and T-shirts were holding signs, protesting something. He didn't know what, nor did he care.

"You had your time," he grumbled to himself, as he thought of the protests of the sixties. Those days were long ago and far away, now just a distant, unpleasant memory. The limo pulled past the protesters as the chief looked out with a scowl.

When he arrived at the conference, he was eager to give his speech. He had accepted the invitation to appear immediately and knew exactly what he wanted to say. With great fanfare he was finally introduced and took the podium, bellowing his speech in his deep, rich baritone.

"As you know, the federal judiciary faces a crisis created by larger and larger caseloads.

"Every year we find ourselves having to decide more and more cases, and there is no relief in sight. As our caseloads increase, there is the very real danger that each case will receive less attention than would otherwise be appropriate for well-thought-out decisions.

"In addition to cases involving issues of great importance, where millions of dollars or deep questions of personal morality are at stake, we increasingly find ourselves having to consider cases, many of which are filed by indigent prisoners which are patently absurd or involve matters of minor importance.

"That is why, as many of you already know, we have proposed rules that will deter such filings and other litigation that is not deserving of our attention by imposing stiff penalties against such parties and their attorneys when such cases are brought before the courts for consideration.

"But my topic here today is not the need for sanctions against attorneys and litigants who are taking up the time of the courts with frivolous and minor claims. I am deeply concerned about the quality of legal education in America today. Many of the lawyers I have the misfortune to have appear before me are ill-prepared and ill-equipped to handle the case for which they are responsible. In my estimation, nearly 50 percent of the lawyers appearing in court are either incompetent or have serious deficiencies. More importantly, we have failed to instill in young lawyers, and perhaps our young people in general, a sense of decorum and ethical propriety that leads new lawyers to take positions and cases that do not merit our attention.

"So I call upon legal educators everywhere to stem this rising tide of incompetence and unethical conduct by taking steps to control the behavior of new lawyers through proper instruction and discipline at our many fine law schools throughout this great country, and to do so with all deliberate speed."

The chief continued his speech, receiving polite applause when he had finished. He was not particularly popular within the legal community nor the general public, but because of his position, his opinions drew a great deal of attention. Unlike his predecessors, he was more than willing to express himself in order to influence popular opinion, even though in the minds of many this created the unseemly impression that the chief was now increasingly drawing the Supreme Court into the political arena where as a matter of tradition, not to mention constitutional law, the Court as an institution had dared not enter.

On the evening news the remarks of the chief justice were mentioned briefly.

The next day newspapers across the country quoted Moorehead's speech, particularly his lament at the pervasive incompetence of attorneys.

CHAPTER IX
RADIO WAVES

Earl walked down the stairs slowly, still groggy from sleeping late. He had stayed up late working on his project before finally falling into a fitful sleep. He passed the dining room table on his way to the kitchen, averting his eyes from the mass of papers, books, and assorted pens and highlighters that surrounded his typewriter, a grim reminder of the previous night's paper chase.

Waiting for the coffee to brew, he noticed for the first time how quiet things were. He strained against the silence that pressed against his eardrums, trying to detect some sign of life.

There was none.

All of his classmates had already fled the jurisdiction for their real homes, eager to enjoy the winter holidays with their families. Although he had finished his final exams and was free to go, Earl had decided to linger in the peace and quiet for a few days. Cup in hand he made his way into the living room, still avoiding the mess on the dining room table.

He wasn't awake enough yet to deal with that.

He just sat there a few minutes, waiting for his coffee to cool. The silence was so overwhelming, he could almost detect a humming sensation in his ears, but there was no sound. He was feeling very peaceful, but also very alone. Looking out the window at the greenery and trees, his mind wandered back through his years in college and then law school that were now quickly drawing to a close. Images flashed in his mind of keg parties, late night studying. Marilyn.

He was now poised to complete years of hard work and to begin a career as an attorney. But the future was so uncertain. Employment was hard to find except for those students at the top of the class. He was anxious, almost desperate to finish law school, but felt a nagging feeling of unfinished business.

Earl got up from the couch and went to the dining room table, rummaging to find the memorandum from the university that Frank had given him. Reading the document, which had now been marked as an exhibit, he still couldn't believe that the administration of the university would put this in writing.

After recounting that the first year start-up costs and operating expenditures for the radio station would come to approximately $93,000, and that the annual operating expense would amount to about $33,000, the university questioned the "fiscal responsibility" of the project. But then the memo went on to state that the legal department of the university advised the administration that there were "substantial impediments for the administration regarding the exercise of any control over the information disseminated by university students through the medium of radio." With that, the president of the university announced that he had vetoed the idea of the radio station. At the same time he also vetoed the initiative approved by the students that would have used interest from the special funds Frank had discovered for student loans.

Frank was crestfallen when he heard the news. Earl was outraged.

The president of a major university had blocked the funding of a radio station owned, operated, and paid for by students because his administration would be unable to censor the broadcasts of the station. Earlier in the history of the school, the university pulled the funding from the student newspaper because of critical news coverage of decisions made by the administration and the inability to control family planning advertisements run by the paper.

So much for freedom of speech on a college campus, Earl thought to himself.

At the same time the president also managed to utterly crush the appetite of the students to get politically involved. Just when students had been shown a path by which they could make a decision without relying on the whims of their representatives, the president had reminded them of how hopeless the situation really was. Even if you can get something you really want from student government, he was saying, unelected officials of the university really have the final say. He had proved once again that voting doesn't matter, a lesson that has been carried into life beyond the campus where fewer and fewer people bother to make their way to the polls on Election Day.

Earl researched the subject and found that a successful legal challenge to the university could be mounted. But Frank pointed out that student government could not hire a lawyer to take the case. The university would veto paying money to the lawyer. Frank even described how the university had blocked other suits by SG by refusing to pay the lawyers. The power of the purse had given the university the power to deprive students of their freedom of speech, their right to vote, and the right to have an attorney represent them, which meant in effect that the students had no right to have their case heard in court.

Earl felt personally cheated. For years he had labored under the yoke of subjugation by the university, viewing with contempt the hapless student government types who refused to stand up for the students or who actively sold students down the river for their own personal gain. He had grown to accept the cynicism shared by most students and the fact that nothing would ever change. He had allowed himself to feel a ray of hope when the radio station was passed, and then approved by SG, only to have this blooming optimism crushed by an administration bent on imposing the oppressive atmosphere of cynicism that gave the president free reign over the students. Earl was convinced that other students also had their hopes raised, and dashed, vowing never again to allow themselves to believe that things could be different and that they could help make a difference.

Something inside of Earl made him want to fight back. He had an instinctive feeling that triggered a deep desire to see justice done. He felt somehow responsible for vindicating the rights of the students, as if they had placed trust in him, just as he had placed trust in the system. To do nothing in the face of this outrage was to condone what the university had done, to accept impotence and cynicism as a way of life.

Earl didn't have the money to hire a lawyer. But he used the one resource available to find a way to fight back. He spent hours in the law library trying to find a way to circumvent the box into which the administration had placed SG. His research centered on "pro-sers" – people who represent themselves in court, which he had learned about in a course on police practices. Most "pro-sers" are what are commonly referred to as "jailhouse lawyers," people who have several years with nothing better to do than read thousands of volumes of law books in the vain attempt to find some sort of loophole to set them free.

The course in police practices inspired Earl to re-read a book about Clarence Earl Gideon, a poor man who, while spending his time in jail, wrote his own petition to the Supreme Court, called a petition for certiorari, or cert petition, asking that his case be heard on the grounds that he was too poor to hire an attorney. The handwritten paper was actually what in legal terminology would be described as "frivolous" because the court had already ruled that a poor man such as Gideon had no constitutional right to have a lawyer represent him in a criminal case at the expense of the state.

But the Supreme Court took his case, reversed the prior ruling, and established what is today the common right of all people to have an attorney in a criminal case when they are unable to afford one.

The story of Gideon was a moving example of the struggle of the oppressed against a sometimes unfair system, and was a real example of how a common man of modest means was able to help himself and in the process establish an important right for others. But the right to counsel did not apply in civil cases. This left those people, such as Earl, who could not afford a lawyer in a civil case to represent themselves.

The Supreme Court of the United States had decided that not only may a person represent themselves in a criminal matter, they have the *constitutional right* to do so, a decision that the justices of the Supreme Court have probably regretted from that day forward. In theory, the courts are open to any person who manages to stagger into the courthouse with gibberish written on a piece of toilet paper, which the clerk of the court is duty bound to file stamp and docket as a pending case. In practice, because of the abundance of crackpots and other assorted escapees from the mainstream of society who regularly exercise this constitutional right, few pro-se litigants get very far in the courts, even if the case in question has merit.

Many people who find themselves in this position simply do not have the means to hire an attorney. While the very poor may qualify for the limited legal aid programs available for some types of cases, the vast majority of working poor and middle class in America today make too much to qualify for legal aid and too little to afford their own attorney. Of course, many other pro-se individuals have the means but not the inclination to get a lawyer, as they prefer the satisfaction of fighting their own battles. These types of litigants also usually distrust all lawyers (apparently without considering that the judge hearing the case is also an attorney).

Judges, although required by law to humor pro-se litigators, seem to have a bias against anyone foolish enough to hire themselves as their own attorney.

Earl did not pause long to consider that in practicality a lawsuit where he represented himself would go nowhere. He had found a way to fight back. As a student who had voted on the radio station and as a person who was deprived of the right to hear the broadcasts, as opposed to the broadcaster, he had the right, called "standing," to challenge what the university had done. Since the university had blatantly imposed censorship of free speech under the authority of the state-run university system, the school could be held liable for violation of the First Amendment to the Constitution.

Earl put his coffee cup down and flipped through the crude lawsuit he had drafted, complete with exhibits and what he thought was appropriately legal-sounding words and phrases. The suit was much more difficult to prepare than his other papers in the traffic case. But technically, the form of the paper was not that important as long as his legal theory was correct.

He put the lawsuit down and made his way into the kitchen for another cup of coffee. He watched a squirrel out the window. He sipped from the steaming cup, thinking about Marilyn and how much he had already started to miss her. Then his thoughts returned to this crazy lawsuit and the right, he asserted, to hear. The silence in the room was beginning to take on a special significance. He walked back into the living room and turned on the record player for some music.

He decided to just replay the record that was still on the turntable, a rendition of Beethoven's sixth symphony conducted by Leonard Bernstein.

As the soothing music filled the room, a sudden feeling of melancholy overcame Earl. He thought about the cruel irony of the great composer's progressive loss of hearing. He tried to imagine how he must have felt, being deprived of the ability to enjoy something so important in his life. The thought made him appreciate those sounds even more.

The next day Earl passed through the doors of the downtown state court building, clutching his papers to his side. The lobby of the courthouse was sterile and uninviting. A guard near the front entrance directed him to the clerk's office on the right side of the lobby. He walked to the glass doors leading into a small enclosed area. Straight ahead was a window opening with a counter behind which stood a court clerk.

The clerk was an older woman with a look of disapproval that had apparently been frozen into place after years of dealing with the general public. She was a vision reminiscent of a typical librarian, complete with graying hair and unassuming attire. Earl approached the counter with trepidation. He placed his lawsuit and other papers on the counter and asked her if this was the proper place to file his lawsuit. She stared down at him over her classic bifocals and paused briefly, apparently sizing him up.

"I'm sorry. I can't give out legal advice."

"But I'm not asking for legal advice; I'm just asking if this is where to file my suit."

"That is a legal question, young man. You will have to consult a lawyer to find out which court has jurisdiction over this particular case."

"Okay, look, I'll make this easier for you. Is this the clerk's office for the circuit court?"

"Yes, of course it is."

"Good. Here is the complaint I want to file."

"One moment, please."

She had suddenly become very busy shuffling papers and filing files. Earl waited patiently, leaning conspicuously against the counter and into the inner sanctum. Behind the counter where the clerks met their public was a scene typical of any government bureaucracy, complete with bland desks and chairs and rows of filing cabinets. He greeted clerks as they walked near the opening at the counter, keeping his eye on the librarian. She would occasionally glance up, and he would smile sweetly at her. Finally, after several minutes of suffering his presence, she pulled out a blank file folder with an audible sigh and returned to the counter.

She looked at the papers and then at Earl. "Are you sure you want to do this?"

He was taken aback by this question. *What did she mean?* He nodded his head, watching her carefully. With a slight shrug of her shoulders, she began to shuffle the papers, stamping this and marking that with a flourish. Then she closed the file folder and looked up at Earl.

"All right. Your case has been filed with the court."

"Thank you. I need to see the judge right away."

"I'm sorry, I can't help you. That would be giving out legal advice."

"Well, do you think it would be all right to tell me who the judge is on my case?"

"Judge Oliver," she replied without batting an eye.

"Thank you."

Earl took his lawsuit and wandered away from the counter. He stood to the side, a large column partly blocking his view of the counter area where the librarian continued about her business. A young woman approached the counter. She was apparently some sort of paralegal. He listened as the librarian greeted her warmly and suddenly became a wellspring of information.

I'd ask her where the bathroom is, he thought to himself as he went back through the glass doors and into the lobby, *but I suppose that would be giving out legal advice.* He went back to the guard and asked for directions to Judge Oliver's chambers.

In the elevator he couldn't drive thoughts about *Oliver Twist* from his mind. Pictures of greasy boys with holes at the tips of their gloves were going through his mind when the elevator doors opened, and he walked to the secretary's desk.

"Is this Judge Oliver's chambers?"

"Yes, it is. May I help you?"

He handed her his lawsuit. "I need to see the judge right away on this case."

She looked at him and asked him to sit down while she took the file in to the judge. He waited for what seemed like an eternity. At last, the judge called him into chambers. The judge sat behind his desk, reading over the papers thoughtfully.

"What is this all about?" he asked suddenly.

"The university is preventing a student-run radio station from broadcasting because the president of the university wants to censor any broadcasts by the station. That is a violation of the First Amendment and is a prior restraint of free speech."

"What is it that you want me to do?"

"I need an injunction to prevent the university from interfering with setting up the radio station."

The word "injunction" nearly brought the judge to his feet. "I'm not issuing an injunction."

"But, Judge–"

"Forget it. There is no way I am going to grant an injunction against the university. Besides, you have not served them with these papers. I don't want them to be deprived of due process, you know." With that, the judge made some sort of notation on the inside cover of the court file, and then shooed Earl out of his office. Dazed, Earl stumbled out of the judge's office, into the elevator, and through the lobby towards the main entrance to the courthouse, smiling weakly at the guard who had been so helpful to him during his little visit to the court.

As if in a trance, he boarded the bus and plopped down on the seat in the rear. His experience in court was not quite what he had expected, although he didn't know what to expect. He had the vague feeling that he had been given the old bureaucratic shuffle.

Were courts really just glorified bureaucracies? he thought to himself.

The judge's reaction was curious. Did he mean to say that the idea of granting an injunction itself was just so far out of the question as to be absurd, regardless of the merits of the case? He seemed to be guided by some inner voice or gut level reflex and not by the law.

There was much about the law that Earl had no way of knowing. He knew the rules well by now, but the rules didn't tell him that he was supposed to set a hearing with the judge, make a notice of the hearing, and send a copy to the lawyers for the university. He thought that a hearing would be set by the judge automatically. So like other pro-se litigators, he had to go back to the books and figure out what to do next.

His research at the law library that afternoon revealed that he had a real problem. The judge did not write an order denying his injunction. Under the rules he could not appeal the judge's decision unless the ruling was in writing and filed with the clerk of the court. He found no case saying notes scribbled on the cover of the file qualified as a written, appealable order.

What Earl didn't know is that there was another unwritten rule that says that the attorneys in a case are the ones who write the orders that judges sign, a fact that is not common knowledge and would probably come as somewhat of a shock to the average person. Had he known this, he could have written an order that denied his own motion, giving him something that he could appeal. But there was no one there to tell him these unwritten rules. That would be giving "legal advice."

The fact that the judge did not issue a written order denying his injunction left Earl in a sort of legal limbo. This meant that he could not file an appeal to the court of appeals in Tallahassee, the state capital, or the Florida Supreme Court. Usually, he would be expected to pursue his case in those courts after being denied by the trial judge. But he couldn't.

At home that night Earl sat down at the dining room table and read over his research one last time. The statute on jurisdiction said that a party had to seek redress in the highest state court in which a decision could be reached before an appeal could be made to the United States Supreme Court. Under the circumstances, he had, in effect, gone to the highest court where a decision could be had. There was no further appeal in the state court system beyond Judge Oliver's ruling.

Earl pulled out a sheet of paper. At the top of the paper after the address, he wrote what he thought would be an appropriate salutation:

"Dear Whomever Reads the Supreme Court's Mail:"

CHAPTER X
ROUND ONE

The clerk's office at the U.S. Supreme Court receives thousands of cert petitions every year, most of which are from indigent prisoners.

Although the clerk was designed as a ministerial office that simply performs the mechanical function of filing papers and docketing cases, the chief had gradually converted the clerks into the first line of defense against the flood of papers being sent to the court from the prisons of the nation. With the new role of the clerk as part of the screening process, there would be fewer chances of a new Gideon to find his way into the chambers of the justices, but the justices would be relieved of some of their burden.

Earl's papers arrived along with stacks of other papers and printed briefs from attorneys, law firms, and governments. The clerk who opened his package barely stopped long enough to roll her eyes skyward at his unusual salutation. She scanned the paper and saw that no appeal had been taken from the order of Judge Oliver. She immediately sent the papers back to Earl with an explanation that she could not file them because the court lacked jurisdiction. She wrote that he had not obtained a decision in the highest court in which a decision could be had.

She became a little annoyed when she received the papers from Earl again a few days later. Earl tried to explain his legal position to her again. He even went so far as to file an appeal in the state court of appeals, knowing that they would dismiss the appeal, to prove that he had already gone to the highest state court in which a decision could be had. After some confusion because there was no order to appeal, the trial court clerk informed the appeals court that there was no order and, after checking with Judge Oliver, that there would be no order entered that could be appealed.

But when the clerk received his papers, she sent them back again, noting that an appeal was still pending in the state court of appeals. She refused to file them with the court. Exasperated, Earl wrote a letter to the chief justice to explain the situation. He complained that the clerk's office had usurped the judicial power of the court to decide whether the court had jurisdiction of a case by refusing to docket his case. By that time he had received the order from the state court of appeals dismissing his appeal because there was no appealable order, confirming what he had been trying to explain all along.

The letter to the chief had been routed directly to the clerk who had been sending his papers back. She was appalled and now a little more than annoyed at Earl. She resented the endless stacks of pro se papers that never got anywhere with the court anyway. Grumbling something under her breath, she docketed the case and sent a notice to Earl giving him the case number and a form to enter his appearance before the Supreme Court.

Earl's emergency papers were sent up to a group of clerks with reams of other pro se papers that had made their way past the clerk's office. After a response was filed by the attorneys for the university, the case file was deposited on the desk of Ron Meyers, one of the law clerks assigned to review papers filed pro se. As with other cases on the "paid" docket (most pro se litigants were given indigent status and allowed to proceed without paying the $200 filing fee and having their papers professionally printed, which cost hundreds of dollars), the pro se papers were read by the clerks and a summary was prepared giving the justices a brief overview of the case. This relieved the justices from having to waste their time plowing through thousands of pages of cert petitions, which in the case of pro se petitioners contained little more than gibberish.

Meyers picked up Earl's file with an audible sigh. He had just finished a summary in a case where the petitioner argued that the state court had no jurisdiction in his case because the judge had a flag with yellow trim hanging in his office. Since the flag was an old maritime flag donated from the U.S. Navy, he reasoned that the judge was hearing the case in admiralty. Everyone knows that admiralty cases can only be heard in federal court, so the judge in the state court had no jurisdiction the petitioner concluded triumphantly.

Meyers immediately noticed that Earl's papers were different from most of the other pro se papers. The petition and motions were neatly typed and contained citations to authorities that complied with the proper legal form. But Meyers had been there long enough to find that occasionally the court would receive neatly typed papers where the petitioner was being pursued by aliens or the CIA or both. He had yet to find a pro se petition that was marginally meritorious, and the court in his experience had yet to agree to hear a single one of these cases.

After reading over the papers, he realized that this case would need special attention. He put the file in his briefcase to take home that night and headed for the library to do some research. As he looked up the cases cited by Earl and did some research of his own, he discovered that he had a problem. For the first time he had a pro se petition with issues of sufficient substance to actually make the Court agree to hear this case. But he remembered the lecture given to him by the chief justice. In writing cert summaries in pro se cases, he was not to try and find an issue worthy of the Court's consideration, even if he found such an issue in a particular case. He was to make the summaries as short as possible so as not to waste the time of the Court. The chief made the distinct impression that he did not want a single pro se case heard by the Court and had taken a public stand that all such cases were frivolous.

From a reading of Earl's papers, Meyers knew that the case at least had arguable merit. Had the case been brought by a lawyer or some group like the ACLU, the Court would probably grant the petition and might even rule in Earl's favor on the merits. The thought gave him a chill. He had only been working there a few months and didn't want to lose his job. Besides, if this guy got his petition granted, every loony tune in the country would be encouraged to file cert petitions, flooding the court with papers he would have to plow through.

At home that night Meyers carefully drew up a summary that he thought would be innocuous enough to escape notice. He also chose his words to give the case a little slant in favor of the university. He wrote that the petitioner "claims that the reason for not expending what are undoubtedly scarce resources of the university was because of 'censorship' of the broadcasts by the proposed student-run radio station." He had seen the memo from the university admitting to the censorship but was betting that none of the justices would bother to look at the court file. He knew that the fiscal scarcity comment would appeal to the conservative justices on the Court.

He also left out Earl's argument that the actions of the university, approved by the judge who failed to act, amounted to a "prior restraint" of free speech. A prior restraint triggered a strict legal standard adopted by the court which presumed that the restraint was illegal and which required that the courts, including the Supreme Court, give expedited review to such cases. Meyers also emphasized that the trial judge did not make a ruling without mentioning that Judge Oliver had refused to sign a written order apparently precisely to avoid an appeal and that Earl had not sought review up to the Florida Supreme Court.

By the time Meyers was finished, the summary made Earl's case sound pathetic. He had managed to depict a case with merit as being ludicrous. As a finishing touch he noted that "not surprisingly" the university had filed papers against Earl asking that fines be levied against him for filing a "frivolous" case.

The cert summary in Earl's case circulated along with hundreds of others in the chambers of the nine justices. The justices would review the summaries and meet on a regular basis to vote on which cases would be heard by the court. A petition for cert would be granted if four of the nine justices voted in favor of doing so. Pro se petitions were denied usually en masse at these meetings, unless a justice asked that a vote be taken on a particular case.

Meyers' summary of Earl's case had the desired effect of passing largely unnoticed through the chambers of the justices, although law clerks pointed out the special significance of the petitioner's name.

The summary did not escape the notice of Chief Justice Moorehead.

At the cert conference all of the other justices had voted to deny cert in all of the pro se cases listed for that day, which included the "admiralty" case and Earl's case. Then the time came for the chief to vote.

"I agree that we should deny cert in all of these cases, but I would also vote to grant the motion for sanctions in the Warren case. The case is obviously frivolous, causing the university to expend resources answering this litigation. They should be compensated, and granting sanctions against some of these people would be a lesson to other parties who may seek to file papers that take up the time of this Court."

The conference room was silent for a moment. For years the court had taken a tolerant view towards the hapless pro se petitioners who filed their bizarre claims in the Court. The Court rarely granted such motions, and to start doing so now would actually increase the amount of time spent on the cases when they could very easily dispose of the cases in a single, one-sentence order denying the petition for cert. The chief obviously had an ax to grind and was willing to have the whole Court pay the price for his crusade against frivolous litigation.

Baker was the first to speak.

"Chief, don't you think it would be better to just deny the cert petition and move on to the other cases? We don't want to start deciding sanctions every time someone asks for them, or we will end up spending all our time hearing these motions."

Two other justices immediately nodded in agreement. Baker became alarmed when he noticed that the others did not take an immediate stand. He feared that they might go along with the chief to keep him happy. Some were counting on his vote in their cases, others wanted decent assignments. They were not willing to make an issue out of such a trivial matter.

"Perhaps we should carry this case to the next conference, Chief," Baker finally said. "To be honest, I wasn't prepared for a vote on the motion for sanctions in this case and would like to study the issue before making a decision." The other justices nodded in agreement.

"Very well," said the chief, trying to hide his displeasure. He didn't want Baker to start lobbying the others about this case and had almost succeeded in his surprise attack. But he did not want to lose on this in front of the others, and he could see that they all agreed to postpone the vote.

Back in his chambers Baker was mortified. He had his secretary bring in a copy of the cert summary in Earl's case. When he read the paper, he noticed for the first time that the petitioner shared the name with the great chief justice whose standing in legal circles made Moorehead cringe with envy. But that was not enough to set Moorehead off about this case. As he read the summary again carefully, he remembered thinking that the case had some substance on the merits. He had decided to deny cert because the procedural issues were too sticky. He called in one of his clerks to check the original papers in the court file.

Meanwhile, in Moorehead's chambers, the chief was fuming with anger. He was determined to strike back at this college student trying to relive the sixties. This punk had the gall to take on the university and to bring his little "protest" into *his* domain. He wanted to teach this kid a lesson he would never forget. He started by putting together a memo to circulate to the other justices on how the Court was overworked and the need to make a statement about frivolous filings. These pro se people had gotten away with too much for too long, and he did not want them to think they had free reign in his court.

After being briefed by his clerk, Baker started on a memo of his own. He was getting a little bit angry himself, and the feeling was giving him some momentum. The changing of the guard at the Court had made him depressed. He had even considered resigning. But he was beginning to feel his oats, and he was ready to meet the challenge head-on. He had no intention of letting this great institution turn into the personal fiefdom of one man bent on turning the clock back to the good old days of segregation and unchecked government power, closing the door on the downtrodden and weak without even giving them the right to have their cases considered by the Court.

When Wade read the competing memos, he could see that the two justices were on a collision course. The chief was still on his crusade to punish the pro se petitioners, making an example of this college kid. Baker had gone off the deep end, announcing that not only would he deny sanctions but had reconsidered and now wanted to vote to grant cert in the case. The clash of these two egos, if made public, would damage the prestige of the Court, all over a pro se case with marginal merit at best. Wade decided that as a moderate on the Court he should try to broker a compromise.

Wade had had his own clerk write up a memo on the case. The primary case relied upon by Earl was the "black arm-band case," where a group of college students in the sixties wanted to wear black arm bands as a protest. The university tried to stop them. The Court sided with the students in an opinion which stated that the Constitution was not something that was "checked in" at the schoolhouse gate. The decision was a ringing endorsement of the right of students to speak on campus.

Earl's case on the facts was not the same, but the basic principle was. Wade saw that the case did have merit but was not quite as perturbed as Baker at the distortions in the cert summary prepared by Meyers. The summaries were not supposed to be slanted or argumentative, but he could understand how a clerk who spent all day every day reading cert petitions, almost all of which were ridiculous, might write up a summary that did not give the benefit of the doubt to the pro se petitioner.

Wade struck upon a plan to resolve the tempest in a teapot that was about to get out of hand. He drafted a memo that agreed that the case on the merits would likely be found by the Court to be a violation of the First Amendment but that he had a problem with jurisdiction. Earl had relied partly on a case where the Court had agreed to hear whether a Nazi group could march in a predominantly Jewish area of a small town. The case had been heard by the Court before the state courts had a chance to give the case full consideration. The Court should be leery of expanding this jurisdiction beyond limited cases of extreme emergency. Earl could always go back to the state courts and get a ruling that could be appealed at a later time, Wade wrote.

He didn't mention the issue of sanctions, hoping that when the chief saw two justices agreeing with Earl on the merits, he would have to concede that the case wasn't "frivolous." Before the next conference, Wade made a point of coming to see Baker in his chambers to discuss the case.

"I know you have strong feelings about this case," he said after they had exchanged greetings.

"That cert summary is typical of what the chief has done to this Court," Baker countered before Wade could continue. "He thinks that the only important cases are when a major corporation is involved or the police want greater power to search civilians without a warrant. He has no right to undermine the way this Court makes decisions because of his agenda."

"I know, I know. But you also have to admit that almost all of these pro se cases are frivolous."

"What about cases like Gideon v. Wainwright? That was a pro-se case, too, you know.

"Think where we would be today if that case had been screened out, or a man like Gideon was afraid to petition this Court to hear his case because he was afraid that he would be fined, or worse. Are we going to get to the point where we start adding time to prisoners who dare to write to us?"

"I agree, but keep in mind that we all voted to deny cert in this case, yourself included. Don't make this into an issue with the chief when you know we should deny cert anyway."

"I'm not so sure that we should."

"Look, I haven't taken a head count yet, but I think that even if you can convince three others to go along with you on granting cert, I'm not sure what the outcome would be on the merits. I think we'd end up dismissing the case on jurisdictional grounds. Then what would you have accomplished? You might even end up with a majority tinkering with the black arm-band case and the right of students to speak on campus."

Baker looked at his colleague for a moment. Wade was right. He didn't want to make waves over a silly pro se case. Besides, he was hoping to get Wade to write a good opinion in that school busing case and didn't want to offend him. "Okay, I get the drift," he said with a smile. "But I'm not going along with sanctions. I'll write a dissent if that happens."

"Don't worry about that," Wade replied, relieved.

At the next cert conference, Moorehead looked tense. As the vote was taken on Earl's case, three justices had, surprisingly, voted to grant cert in the case by the time Baker was to vote. He sensed that some of the justices were looking to use this case to limit the scope of freedom of speech on campus or erode the Court's right to hear such cases on an expedited basis.

"I know this may come as somewhat of a shock," said Baker, "but I'm going to vote to deny cert. Even if there are four votes to hear the case, we would eventually dismiss the case, cert having been improvidently granted. The jurisdictional issue here seems to me to be dispositive, as I had originally thought when the case first came up for a vote."

The chief seemed perplexed. He was also trapped. He could not vote to grant cert in a case he thought was frivolous. But he could hardly argue a case as being frivolous when three other justices agreed to hear the case.

"I vote to deny cert, obviously," he said grimly. "Now, what about the issue of sanctions?" After a brief uncomfortable silence, Wade went first.

"Well, I voted to deny cert, as you know. But since three of my brethren voted to grant cert, I do not see how I can now say the case is frivolous." He paused for a split second before continuing, "Even if I were of such a view." All of the other justices agreed. Then the time came for the chief to vote on the motion for sanctions.

"Well then, the motion is denied," said the chief, his face ashen. No one commented on the fact that he didn't announce his own vote on the motion.

At the law school Earl waited until he got into the smoking room to open the form letter he had received from the United States Supreme Court. He had no idea of the struggle that had taken place over his case. The letter was the only communication he had received from the Court other than the notice that his case had

been docketed. He opened the letter which simply said:

"The motion of respondent for sanctions is
denied. The petition for a writ of certiorari is
denied."

CHAPTER XI
THE GRADUATE

Earl made his way through the hallway to his class on environmental law. A student smiled and waved to him as he passed. He returned the smile with a nod and mumbled a "how ya doin'" as he passed her. He didn't recall ever having met her before. This scene had been repeated numerous times, although much less so now that the furor (and publicity) about his suit against the university had receded.

When the suit was first filed, Frank had called a reporter for the local newspaper and the paper published by the students, the one which had been kicked off campus years ago. He was very forthcoming and cooperative with the press but felt a little ill at ease, particularly when the articles were published. Aside for the minor errors of fact, such as his age and his school classification (he was 3LW, not 2LW), he was struck with the distorted image the articles had created. Not that the image was bad. The student paper in particular nearly lionized him in his crusade against the university. But for a person who is so familiar with the facts and circumstances of an event to read a necessarily brief account of that event in the paper reveals how little information is really conveyed in a newspaper article. Earl began to wonder about the missing details, errors of fact, and distortions in articles he had read throughout his life.

The publicity had made Earl a mini celebrity on campus. The experience was not pleasant.

Earl was a person who always kept to himself, bordering on being completely antisocial. He felt very uncomfortable with the way people would stare, or point in his direction and whisper to another student. Privacy was a right he had taken for granted. Now that that right had been ripped aside, he began to regret the whole idea of making waves on such a public level. He had paranoid feelings that everyone was looking at him and talking about him, and for good reason.

People *were* looking at him and talking about him.

He was glad that things had begun to die down. He just wanted this ordeal to be behind him. When he got the order from the Supreme Court, he was more relieved than disappointed. He had no way of knowing that the lawsuit against the university was to have a much greater impact on his life for years to come. But for now, he was in his last semester and was looking forward to finishing his stint in law school.

Frank caught up to Earl and took him gently by the arm, guiding him to a bench.

"Mr. Chief Justice, how are things up there in the Supreme Court these days? I know you're an authority on the subject."

"Not anymore, Frank," Earl replied with a sigh. "Guess what happened?"

"I'm afraid to ask."

"You know that initiative that was passed by the students on the Lake Wigwam project? The one that the university vetoed?"

"How could I forget?"

Student government had agreed to pay nearly a quarter of a million dollars of student money for repairs to the lake requested by the university. The repairs, which were for improving property owned by the university, had drawn fire from students because funds for such capital improvements were available from a fund established by the legislature. In a referendum passed by students ala Solidarity, the money for the repairs was rejected by student government. True to form, the university vetoed the initiative and took the money anyway.

"Well, Ralph and Mark, following your lead, went down to the court and filed their own lawsuit to reverse this decision. But the judge laughed them out of court. Said they did not serve the university and dismissed their case. How do you like that?"

"I don't. Those bastards pulled the plug on the radio station, saying there was not enough money. And now when the time comes to spend even more money on something that directly benefits them, they force students to pay for something that they don't want. Fiscal responsibility has nothing to do with it. It's who has the power to control the finances of the students.

"And it's something more, Frank. It's subjugation. It's domination over the will of the students. This is just another slap in the face of students and young people in general. I really believe that the youth in this country are a minority that is discriminated against. The rights of young people, even the right to vote, is restricted purely because of age. Older people think that all kids and young adults should be completely under their domination and control, with no rights and no freedom to make at least some of their own decisions. But I've seen plenty of young people, even little kids, with more intelligence and maturity than many adults."

Earl paused in his speech to see Frank's reaction. He knew that his views were far out of the mainstream but had now realized the underlying problem with the way the university, and society at large, treat young people. In the law, people who are deprived of the right to vote and are regarded as something less than people are called an "insular minority" because they are insulated from the normal political and other processes through which decisions are made and actions taken that affect everyday lives. Laws passed or enforced on the basis of a trait associated with such an insular minority might be declared unconstitutional for being "discriminatory".

A court of law is the one place that members of such an insular minority can seek refuge.

But Earl and now Frank's cohorts were having difficulty making the court system respond to protect the rights of young people, who are a classic insular minority deserving of greater judicial scrutiny of laws that adversely affect them. There was no doubt that the university was ready, willing, and able to directly and explicitly violate the right of students to speak, to vote, to hire an attorney to represent them, or to exercise any other right that would be taken for granted when sought by an adult. Unfortunately, the courts were manned by the same people who, by force of practice over centuries, did not even stop to question if the sacrifice of these rights in the case of young people was really justified.

The prospect that this situation would soon be rectified was nonexistent. By the time a member of this minority group is in a position of power to decide the matter, such as a judge or head of a major university, he or she has become through the process of aging a member of the majority of adults, assuming the same inherent bias against the rights of young people that have been passed down through the ages.

The result is that by the time young people pass into the ranks of adulthood, they have been conditioned to live their entire lives without responsibility. Then, at the stroke of midnight on their 18th birthday, they become a real person with the weight of adult decision-making on their shoulders and with virtually no preparation or prior experience, other than to sit helplessly and watch as bad decisions are made for them by others. The cumulative effect over the years has been to create a mass of people who are apathetic, cynical, and unresponsive to the qualities associated with good citizenship.

"I knew how you would react," Frank said during Earl's pause. "What are you going to do?"

Earl turned melancholy. "Unfortunately, after I graduate there is a real good chance the university can get my case dismissed for lack of standing. Unless I become a career student or can pass the torch to a succession of future students to be the plaintiff in this suit, there really isn't anything I *can* do. That's part of the problem."

They looked at each other for a moment in silence. Earl would miss Frank when each had gone their own way. Maybe if they had gotten together sooner, they would have been able to do more before the time came to leave.

"I suppose you're right," Frank said finally. He looked at his watch. "Time for tax law."

"Time for environmental law," Earl answered as they both got up to head for class.

Earl slipped into the back of the class which was in progress. Professor Kaye had already taken attendance and was droning on again about his theory of environmental law. He claimed to be an expert on economic theory which he had adopted for use in deciding whether to enforce a particular restriction on industry to prevent pollution. Under his theory a company would not be forced to comply with a given regulation if the result would run afoul of a cost-benefit analysis. This analysis calls upon the decision-maker to determine whether the cost of a contemplated action outweighs the benefit to be gained by that action. If so, the action is not taken.

A number of students had questioned the soundness of Kaye's theory as applied to environmental regulations. Kaye, who was a young, conservative teacher, bitter about being denied tenure, had a mustache that dominated his weasel-like features. He would respond with disdain to these questions by explaining that all economic theory took certain assumptions to be true which could, of course, be questioned. The theory was just a tool to help make a particular decision, not a substitute for consideration of other factors that may undercut these assumptions.

The class proceeded as usual. Kaye would, after an extended monologue, ask a question of the students or ask for volunteers to explain the next case to the class. He would stand there for several minutes of uncomfortable silence until a student, usually one of a small group trying to impress Kaye, would slowly raise their hand in response. The students didn't like Kaye, a fact of which he was keenly aware. The feeling was mutual.

After Kaye had applied his cost-benefit analysis for the umpteenth time, Earl, who had studied economics extensively during his undergraduate years, raised his hand.

"Yes, Mr. Warren?" Kaye said with a sigh.

"Excuse me, Professor Kaye, but I have a question about your cost-benefit theory. Couldn't you say that if a given pollutant is just too toxic to allow it to spill into the environment, killing millions of people, that the benefit of allowing this pollutant is simply one which would not be permitted at any price as a matter of morality and public policy?"

"Well, as I have said before, there are a number of basic assumptions that one must accept in any economic analysis."

"But, Professor," Earl said before Kaye could continue to repeat his standard line, "my question has nothing to do with the assumptions but the application of the theory itself. To use a well-known example, Ford Motor Company may decide that it is cheaper to pay people injured by cars that they know explode on impact than to fix the defect in the car. This may make sense economically, but the law is designed to enforce public policy, and it is against public policy to allow a corporation to kill and maim innocent people, even if it's profitable to do so."

"This is environmental law, Mr. Warren. Consumer law and products liability are down the hall. What does Ford Motor Company have to do with this class?"

"The principle is the same, Professor Kaye. The law must be written so that the cost of polluting the environment is so high that a company applying a cost-benefit analysis would decide that polluting the environment was not worth it. In the case of Ford, if the law imposed a cost to the company for selling defective cars that was greater than the production costs they saved, they would have been forced to fix the cars, rather than selling cars to the public that they knew would injure and kill people."

"But what you fail to grasp, Mr. Warren, is that in this application of cost-benefit analysis, the cost of equipment and devices that may reduce emissions marginally would not be imposed against a company because the benefits derived from these requirements are not enough to justify the closing of a plant or an increase in prices to the consumer."

"But it is often hard to assess the costs of pollution, such as health costs or the intangible cost of a species of bird that has become extinct. And what about someone who gets cancer from the gradual emission of carcinogens into the environment? How can you put a price tag on human life and the suffering of a family whose father has developed cancer?"

"Yes, well, that is a fine sentiment, Mr. Warren; however, in the real world companies and agencies must make hard decisions in a systematic way. For those who are unfamiliar with the way in which economic theory is applied, these decisions may not seem clear. As I have stated previously, there are a number of assumptions made in economic theory which are often overlooked in applying the theory to a given set of circumstances."

Earl sat down slowly as Professor Kaye continued with his memorized speech on economic theory. He had completely missed the point of what Earl had to say. As class was ending, the professor called Earl to the front of the room.

"Yes, Professor Kaye? You wanted to see me?"

"Ah, the honorable Earl Warren. I note that you now have accumulated more than five absences. As you know, unlike most classes, I have a strict policy about this. You are being expelled from this class, Mr. Warren."

Earl was dumbfounded. "I wasn't aware of any such policy, Professor Kaye."

"I announced it the first day of class."

"But I was absent that day."

"Very funny," Kaye responded with a sneer as he put his papers back in his briefcase. Earl was not trying to be funny. He missed the first day during the "drop-add" period when he was still trying to piece together a schedule of classes that would give him enough credits to graduate. He wasn't even signed up for Kaye's class on the first day.

"It's not funny. If you kick me out of this class, I won't be able to graduate this semester. I'll have to stay longer just to make up for your course."

"That's not my problem. I read the papers, Warren. I know you're busy with things other than this class. That's fine. But you haven't shown for class and you're out."

"What does my lawsuit have to do with this class? Look, you may not agree with my politics, but that is no reason to use your power as a teacher to strike back."

"You're right, I don't agree with your politics. And I don't care for students who challenge me in class, either. You don't know a damn thing about economics or the environment. You're just a damn tree hugger. I have no use for you."

"You can't keep me from graduating."

"I told you, that's not my problem."

"I'll make it your problem. I have a right to be in this class. If you try to kick me out, I'll sue your ass! And you can bet I'm going to bring out what you said about my politics and your fragile ego that can't stand it when a student shows how full of shit you really are."

Kaye glared at Earl, his face growing red. His hands were trembling in a mixture of anger and fear. "You'll never be able to prove it," he managed to say with calmness in his voice.

"Try me," Earl said, bringing his face right up to Kaye's. Their eyes locked for a few moments as they stood, staring at each other angrily. Kaye pulled away as the door in the back of the room opened, and students began to enter. He finished putting his papers and books in his briefcase, avoiding eye contact with Earl, who stood there, hands on hips, waiting. Finally, Kaye looked up at him, a forced look of indifference on his face.

"Fine, Mr. Warren. I won't kick you out of the course. But I don't want you to set foot in my classroom." With that, he turned on his heel and walked out.

Earl wandered back to get his books and papers. He felt like he was in a dream. The room took on a surreal quality as he thought about his angry exchange with Kaye. The words had come flying out of his mouth, to his own surprise. He could hardly believe that he had spoken like that to his professor. Even more remarkable was that his threats had worked.

He walked out of class and into the welcomed fresh air. His mind was racing about how he had just narrowly avoided disaster. He couldn't fathom why Kaye had such a vendetta against him. He hadn't said two words all semester. He realized that his lawsuit and the resultant publicity had created an image of himself that had taken on a life of its own. "Tree hugger?" he asked himself out loud as he walked down the hall. A woman in a suit was walking past him.

"I see you're still wearing your leathers," she said.

Earl looked down reflexively at his blue jeans, boots, T-shirt and motorcycle jacket. He looked up and realized that the professional-looking woman in the suit was Becky, the biker.

"Becky, what happened to you? Must be hard riding your bike with all that stuff on."

"I'm interviewing, Earl. Some of us *do* have to get ready for the real world, you know," she added as she walked away. She had a curious expression on her face. She seemed defensive about the sudden change she had undergone and at the same time perturbed that he had yet to see the light.

Earl went to the law review to seek out Marilyn. He always felt very comfortable walking into law review even though he was not part of the elite group of students that worked there. He had become a regular fixture at the law review office through his many visits to see Marilyn. The secretary greeted him with a big smile and hearty hello as he passed by the front desk and down the long hall to Marilyn's cubicle.

"Anybody home?" he asked as he appeared at her doorway. "Hi, Earl. Take a look at this."

She handed him a freshly printed copy of the new journal of international law. Her face was beaming. Earl looked at the journal, studying the table of contents to see what kind of articles had been written. Then he looked up at Marilyn with a nod of approval.

"The virgin issue of the international law journal. Do you realize what a significant achievement this is for you, Marilyn? For years after you have graduated and gone on to private practice, this journal will be published by law students, some of whom may not have made law review but were fortunate enough to have another avenue to write articles. This may even help define the school as a legitimate scholarly center of study in the field of international law. I'm really proud of you. I mean it."

"Thank you, Earl, but this was your idea. And if you hadn't talked me into running for student government, I never would have gotten the seed money for this journal," she said, standing up and putting her arm around him. He enjoyed the afterglow of this moment for a brief while before telling her what had happened with Kaye.

"That bastard," she said. "But at least you managed to keep from being kicked out of his class. Now you'll be able to graduate with the rest of us." She paused for a moment before continuing. "Speaking of graduating, Earl, have you figured out what you are going to do?" She looked at him earnestly.

Since he was a kid, Earl had always wanted to be a lawyer. Now he was a few short weeks away from graduating law school. Soon after that, he would be granted permission to practice law and set loose on society. After years of planning and working, he had reached his goal, but had no idea what he would do next. His experience in law school and recent events had distracted him to the point that he had lost direction. He was not prepared to march out of the school and into a law office somewhere. He couldn't even find an office into which he could march.

"I guess I'm doing something wrong. I've sent resumes to a coupla' dozen places, and I haven't even received the honor of a rejection letter." He looked deep into Marilyn's eyes. "To tell you the truth, I don't know what I'm going to do."

Marilyn returned his gaze with a mixture of concern and anxiousness. Then she looked down, fingering the international law journal as she spoke. "Earl, you know – if you want to, that is – you could come down to Miami. I'm getting a place there with a couple of friends and I can put you up for a while 'til you find something." She paused for a moment. "If you have other plans, I'll understand."

Earl stared at her in astonishment. She was having a hard time reaching out to him. She was offering to help him adjust to the real world. More importantly, she wanted to share part of her life with him, to keep him near as they both ventured forth into the "cold, cruel world" outside the safe walls of the law school.

"Are you kidding?" Earl blurted out. He crouched down and looked up into her eyes. "Marilyn, I don't know what to say. I think that's a great idea. I'm sure there are plenty of jobs in Miami for wayward law grads waiting to take the bar."

She looked up and smiled. Earl stood up suddenly. "This is purely platonic, of course," he said with mock gravity.

"Of course," she said laughing. "What do you think this is, a love-in with former law students? A sort of commune?"

"Marilyn, I don't know how to thank you."

"Just find what you're looking for and be happy. That will make me happy. Now, I guess I better get back to making my outline for my evidence exam, or *I* won't graduate."

"Okay, see you later." He waved and walked back down the hall and out of the law review office. He was still smiling as he made his way to his locker. He was excited about the prospect of heading for the big city. He was relieved and grateful that he at least now had some semblance of a plan for after graduation. But mostly, he was getting that tingling sensation again at the thought of being with Marilyn.

Several weeks later Earl had finished the last of his law school final exams. The pace had been grueling, but he took comfort in the fact that this was the last time he would have to live through this experience. In environmental law Kaye had a question concerning his cost-benefit theory. Earl was ready. He had dug out old economics books and prepared a detailed answer, complete with handwritten graphs and even mathematical equations that proved that the cost-benefit theory, as applied to the facts given by Kaye, was flawed. He then provided his own modified version of the theory to come to a solution to the problem.

He knew that his answer would blow his cover under the blind-grading system. Kaye was sure to recognize the final exam paper as Earl's. But he knew that Kaye would ignore the blind-grading system anyway. He couldn't bring himself to humor Kaye by simply regurgitating his misguided theory on the exam, even for a decent grade in the course, which he knew he wouldn't get anyway. Besides, at this late stage in the game, a poor grade in this class didn't matter too much.

Earl had made a serious miscalculation.

When he stopped by the law school a week later to check the exam results, he stood in the hallway, staring at the grades that were posted on the wall. Next to his Social Security number was the letter "D" followed by an asterisk. At the end of the paper was a notation next to an asterisk:

"The listed grade on the final exam for these students is to be reduced by one full grade, due to lack of attendance."

Earl looked back at the list of Social Security numbers and grades. His was the only one with an asterisk. He stood there, unable to move for several minutes, his mouth agape. Kaye had flunked him, meaning he did not have the credits to graduate. He would have to enroll in the summer semester, pay for new classes and books, not to mention living expenses, and would have to wait three months to graduate. He also wouldn't leave with Marilyn to set up housekeeping.

Kaye had really screwed him.

He bolted up the stairs to Kaye's office. The door was locked. Earl shook the door knob violently anyway. Then he saw a notice next to the door. Kaye had already left the school for a teaching position at another school, where he could torture a new set of students. He apparently got tired of trying to get tenure at this school. Earl sat down in the stairwell, his head in his hands. He had conditioned all of his mind and his emotions towards the thought that law school was finished and he was starting a new life. The thought carried him through this last grueling set of exams like a beacon of hope. Helplessness, rage, and grief welled up inside of him. He couldn't face the thought that he would have to prolong this agony.

After a few moments, he got up and walked down to one of the familiar benches. He sat quietly, studying the trees and then the building that he had begun to view as his prison. He knew that he had no choice but to adjust himself to his new reality. He had to recondition his mind to accept the fact that he would be around for one more semester. He had to make the best of the situation. Besides, he had brought this upon himself. He had filed a lawsuit that was bound to have repercussions, without stopping to think about what was in his own best interest. Then when Kaye lashed out at him, he didn't swallow his pride and just give him what he wanted on the exam. He had to be cute and shove Kaye's bullshit theory up his ass. Now Kaye had returned the favor and shoved Earl's grades, graduation, and everything else right up *his* ass.

What did he expect?

The following week Earl put on decent slacks and a nice, professional-looking jacket for graduation. Marilyn had been very sympathetic and caring when he told her the news. She asked him if he would come to the graduation with her, but would understand if he didn't feel like going. He decided that he would be a sport about the whole thing. He did not want to lapse into sustained self-pity. He also didn't want to put a damper on Marilyn's big day. So he arrived and sat with Marilyn's parents, who had flown in from Miami for the occasion. She made sure they understood that Earl was just a *friend*, which seemed to put them at ease. Her family was quite well off and expected her to only get seriously involved with someone with the right pedigree, something which Earl sorely lacked. But her mother was intensely curious, asking Earl a lot of questions about Marilyn and how they had come to know each other. She seemed genuine in her interest in what he had to say about himself as well.

The ceremony offered the standard bland affair that left the participants bleary-eyed and dazed with long-winded speeches and the endless procession of robed youngsters walking across the stage as their names were called. Each greeted the president of the university, who dutifully shook the hand of each one after the dean had given them their diplomas. As he watched from his seat, Earl couldn't help thinking that he should have been up there with the rest of his friends. He had the vague feeling that he was being punished for his indiscretions. *Those who went along got along* was the lesson he had yet to learn, despite all those years of higher education.

He did not let his misfortune show. This was a moment he knew all of his friends, especially Marilyn, had been looking forward to for a long time. He greeted some of the students, still in caps and gowns, with hardy congratulations and friendly pats on the back. He shook hands with Mark vigorously, giving him a broad grin and a slap on his shoulder.

"Sorry you couldn't be up there with us," Mark said.

"Are you kidding? They wouldn't let me near the president anyway. Would have been a real security risk. They were afraid I would pour blood on his hands or something as a protest. Probably would have sworn out a few restraining orders." Mark just threw back his head and laughed. Earl spotted Frank in the sea of robes and excused himself.

"Well, Counselor, how does it feel?" Earl said as he pumped his friend's hand. Frank just stopped short for a second and stared, speechless. Then he pulled Earl towards him, embracing him in a bear hug. When they parted Frank looked at him, holding Earl's shoulders with both hands, arms outstretched.

"How does it feel? It feels fucking great to get out of this hellhole. Look, Earl, I've been thinking," he said as he put his arm around his friend and started walking. "I landed this job for a small firm in Miami. Maybe when they finally let you loose you can look me up. By that time, maybe I'll have enough pull to get you into the firm."

"You'd do that for me?" Earl asked, touched.

"Sure, why not? You certainly have more experience than the rest of us."

"Yeah, but unfortunately all bad."

"Right now you're one for one, counting your beer case, and you got a stay in your other case. That's not a bad average, considering. But anyway, look me up when you're in Miami. I'd like to go out for a few beers with you even if I can't get you into the firm."

"Thanks, Frank." They had stopped walking and were standing in the dwindling crowd facing each other. He felt a presence and turned to see Becky standing beside him.

"See you later, Earl," Frank said, as Earl nodded towards him. "Earl, about the other day –"

"Congratulations, Becky," he said, before she could finish as he reached forward and gave her a kiss. She blushed slightly.

"Thanks," she said softly.

"Good luck, Becky. I know you'll make one hell of a lawyer no matter what you do. Just let me give you some advice I have learned already: Don't ride your motorcycle to court; you might leave a bad impression."

She laughed as he squeezed her shoulder. She pulled him to her and gave him a short hug.

She looked at him again before walking over to embrace her parents. Earl turned and noticed Marilyn for the first time, standing nearby, looking at him with a curious expression. She had been watching him as he was kissing and hugging Becky. He walked up to her with a grin. She didn't return his smile. After a minute her expression softened and a smile parted her lips.

"So, do I get equal treatment as the biker chicks?"

"Not quite," Earl replied as he gave her a kiss on the lips slightly longer than appropriate for casual acquaintances. She did not pull away. He hugged her afterward for what seemed like a long time. She held on to him tightly. He felt like he could just stand there, holding her for hours. Then he pulled back and gazed into her eyes. He thought he saw a glisten of moisture.

When they parted, they both turned and walked to her parents arm in arm. They were watching them both very carefully.

"Are you sure there isn't something going on here that we should know about?"

"Oh, Mom," Marilyn said, giving her a hug.

CHAPTER XII
THE INQUISITION

Earl stepped through the doors of the Orlando Hilton, carrying his two bags and motorcycle helmet. He stopped near the entrance as his sunglasses fogged over with the sudden change in temperature from the hot summer day outside to the cool interior of the hotel. Putting his bags down for a moment to wipe off his glasses, he surveyed the elegantly appointed lobby. He was vaguely aware that in his motorcycle attire he may seem out of place in such a fancy establishment. But for the moment he was hot and tired from the long ride and was in no mood to worry about the propriety of his mere presence.

He ran his fingers through his hair, which was matted down and wet with sweat from having his head encased inside a helmet for hours under the hot Florida sun. He spotted the men's room and headed across the lobby. He put his bags and helmet down on the shining, squeaky-clean floor of the bathroom and then splashed water on his face, looking into the mirror for a brief inspection before heading back out into the lobby.

He couldn't help but feel a little naughty about being there to stay with Marilyn, even though she went to great lengths to impress upon him that no romance was involved. She had talked her parents into paying to put her up in the hotel for a few days before the bar exam so that she could concentrate on her studies. She told them she needed two adjoining rooms so that she could turn one room into a study area and have another room where she could take a break to relax, eat, and sleep. She wanted Earl to stay in the adjoining room.

Earl needed little prompting to join her at the hotel. She wanted a partner with whom she could study, and could use some company to keep from going stir crazy. Besides, she missed him.

She was working for a judge in Miami while he was stuck for the summer at the law school making up for Kaye's class. The law school had made arrangements for students like Earl to take the bar exam before finishing the semester, to avoid having to wait until the next year to sit for the exam. He knew that he could use this sort of special training away from the tomb at the law school to focus his attention on this exam.

After knocking on Marilyn's door, Earl waited, his heart starting to pound. She opened the door, gave him a quick kiss on the cheek and smile, and breezily beckoned him to come in. She was wearing an old football jersey and baggy pants. Her hair was pinned up on her head, and she was wearing large glasses that gave her the appearance of an owl. A pencil was tucked on her ear. She was obviously dressed to be comfortable, without any concern about how attractive she looked.

Earl thought she was ravishing.

He hobbled into the room with his bags and helmet, plopping down on the bed wearily. His muscles ached and his skin was still clammy, but he was feeling excited. Marilyn was floating around the room, showing him the layout and asking how things were at the old law school. She grabbed his hand and pulled him off the bed and into her room where a stack of books and papers were piled neatly on her table.

"These are the manuals that came with the bar review course I've been taking. I have a few older books and some tapes. You're welcome to use them."

She had enrolled in one of several privately operated courses in how to pass the bar exam, an expensive proposition that Earl could not afford. He knew that the people who could afford to take these types of courses for the bar, and the test to get into law school for that matter, had an advantage over those who didn't. He planned on using these materials as much as possible to prepare for this exam. But first he wanted to take a shower and rest.

After his shower he laid down on the bed, letting his body go limp. He was asleep within minutes. A few hours later he was thrust into consciousness by Marilyn, who was standing on his bed, bouncing up and down.

"Oye, Oye, Oye, Mr. Chief Justice Earl Warren. Time to get up and get to work!" She bounced off the bed and looked at his startled expression. "I ordered up some coffee. The night is still young, you know." She tossed one of the thick manuals on his bed with a thud before going to answer the door.

Earl dragged himself out of bed and sat down at the table in his room with the manual. He was looking through the table of contents when Marilyn came into the room with the tray of coffee.

"That was some wake-up call," he said as she put the tray down next to the opened manual.

"This is not a vacation, Earl. We have a lot of work to do, and I know your study habits. We need to get down to business."

"Okay, okay." He knew she was right. And he appreciated the fact that she was concerned about his welfare. If she wasn't there to motivate him, he may slough off at the law school and not pass this all-important exam. He started to read through the first outline on tort law, sipping his coffee as Marilyn sat on his bed, book in hand.

For the next three days, they became disciples of the bar review manuals. They fell into patterns where they would study for an hour or two, then take a break to order up food, take a nap, or just talk. Occasionally, they would go down to the lobby for dinner or lunch at the restaurant or take a swim in the pool, but they spent most of the time in their rooms reading the outlines over and over, asking each other questions. Sometimes one would fall asleep while the other pressed onward late into the night. Morning, noon, and night became irrelevant demarcations of their time. They passed only from study periods to their breaks and back to study periods, Marilyn usually the one prompting a sometimes reluctant Earl to return to work.

Earl's mind was beginning to rebel against the repetitive readings and re-readings of the outlines. He had gotten to the point where the outlines were no longer of any use. He had absorbed all he could and was just wasting time that was quickly passing away before the morning of D-Day. Then he listened to some of the audio tapes with his Walkman. The tapes featured an earnest young man with a reassuring rap that was encouragement more than actual instruction. The tapes were interesting, but he doubted if they were really beneficial.

The day before the exam, Earl was beginning to feel anxious. He felt as though he had too much to learn and not enough time. He was nearly panic-stricken, flitting from one book to the next to decide on which subject he should focus his dwindling time and attention. He didn't let Marilyn know what he was feeling. She was plodding through methodically as she always did.

Then he decided to spend the entire day taking the sample exams. He started first with multiple-choice questions that were given on the "multistate" portion of the exam. Then he tried his hand at the essay questions. He noted the time and did a dry run with a set of questions that he tried to complete within the time that the book gave for the questions. Then he checked his answers. As he repeated this drill, he saw that he was getting a higher and higher percentage of correct answers each time and was able to answer all of the questions within the time allowed.

By late evening he knew he had to stop. Studying late the night before the exam would be counterproductive. Rest was more important. Besides, he felt that he was as ready as he would ever be. Marilyn agreed, after some hesitation. She even went along with his idea to order up a couple of beers to help them relax.

The beers arrived just as Marilyn was coming out of the shower. Earl put the tray on the nightstand in his room and leaned back on the pillows stacked up against the wall on his bed, beer in hand. Marilyn slipped onto the bed beside him, taking the other bottle of beer from the nightstand. Her breast brushed up against him inadvertently. She was wearing a large white T-shirt that clung to her body. He could plainly see her large firm breasts through the thin material. Her nipples had become hard and were protruding.

Earl looked at her as she laid next to him on her side, legs bent slightly in a pose that could easily have been found on the cover of Cosmo or Playboy magazine. He could feel the arousal welling up from deep inside, uncontrollably. She took a long drink of her beer and sighed before looking over at Earl. He leaned over slowly and their lips met, first gently, then with more force as Earl pulled her closer. He passed his hand over her buttocks and down the side of her leg and was bringing his hand back again when she pulled away.

"No, Earl," she stammered as she bolted up from the bed. "Marilyn, I–"

"I can't do this," she said as she was passing through the doorway into her door. She paused for a moment and looked back at him. "At least not now." She closed the door.

A mixture of emotions was swirling inside Earl as he heard the door close softly. He was frustrated and still felt the lingering effects of sexual desire. But he realized that she was probably right. Had they spent the night making furious love, he knew he at least would be distracted during the exam the next day. He would be unable to concentrate, thinking about the night before with Marilyn. Of course, now he would be thinking about what she said before she left and what would happen with them after the exam. But he was thinking that anyway.

He got a fitful night's sleep before Marilyn rousted him early to go down for breakfast. She tried to pretend nothing happened, but there was a noticeable change between them, a feeling that was quickly overwhelmed by the looming challenge that lay before them. They both felt ready but were still nervous with anticipation.

At the convention center they melded into the crowd of anxious men and women who were there to take the bar. The air was thick with the tension that was so readily apparent on the faces of nearly everyone in the room. Earl squeezed Marilyn's hand. He bade her good luck as they each found their assigned seat, exam booklet and pencils laid out neatly before them. A proctor called the group to order and a hush fell over the room.

After some brief instructions, the proctor noted the time and gave the go-ahead to begin the exam. Once he began, Earl quickly set into a comfortable pace of answering the multiple-choice questions. Much to his surprise, he found the words of the young man on the tape had seeped into his subconscious and gave him a soothing backdrop as he breezed through the pages of the exam booklet. When he reached the end, he searched through the book to make sure he wasn't missing anything. He was so engrossed he had lost track of time but, looking around the room, saw that virtually everyone was still seated. After checking again to make sure he had completed the exam, he realized that he was one of the first to finish. He rose from his seat and headed for the exit. Several people looked up in alarm. He put the booklet in the designated box and headed back to the hotel.

Marilyn met him back in their rooms shortly after he had arrived. They talked excitedly about the day's events. She had finished a few minutes after he did, well before most of the rows of other people in the large conference hall. Their method of studying had paid off. The answers just seemed to flow out of them effortlessly. But they couldn't afford complacency. They had to return the next day for another session, instilled with a sense of confidence that all would go well.

A similar scene played itself out the following day. This time Earl, who had again completed his exam long before almost everyone else, waited outside for Marilyn, who joined him after about a 10-minute wait. They went back to the hotel to check out, drained but excited.

They had to scramble to pack their bags in time to make the extended checkout deadline.

Out in the parking lot, Marilyn watched as Earl strapped his bags onto his motorcycle and got ready for his long journey back to forced exile. He smiled as he pulled and clipped his bungee cords around his bags in the familiar ritual he performed at the start of these motorcycle rides.

"When will you be finished up there?" she asked. He had completed packing and was standing in front of her with his helmet in his hand.

"Let's see. My finals start next week, and they run into the end of the following week. Then I will be released from the prison – and not because of good behavior. I served my time and then some, so they're ready to turn me loose on society."

She paused for a second and looked down. "So are you still coming down to Miami?"

Earl stood for a moment, looking at her as if she were a crazy woman. He reached forward and cupped her face in his hands, lifting her head. "I can't think of any place I'd rather be." He gave her a long kiss and embrace.

"I wish I were coming with you now," he said, as he finally pulled away from her.

"Me, too."

He hopped on his motorcycle and jumped on the kick-start a few times before the engine roared to life. He gave her another smile before putting on his helmet and riding off, as Marilyn stood, watching.

Only three months had passed before they both found themselves together again in the parking lot of another Orlando motel. Earl had finished his classes and graduated. He decided to just pick up his diploma and skip the modest ceremony pieced together for the handful of summer graduates. Both Marilyn and he had scored high on the bar exam. Marilyn's score was two points higher, of course. He was now ready to be formally inducted as a new lawyer, or so he thought.

He received a form letter from the Florida Board of Bar Examiners, the agency that screens potential lawyers. He jokingly referred to them as the Florida Bored of Bar Examiners, but the letter he received was no laughing matter. Even though he had completed all of the requirements to become a lawyer – including an undergraduate degree, law school, and passing the bar exam – the board notified him that he would not be admitted, pending an investigation into his character.

Every person seeking the right to practice law in the state of Florida must submit an application, and a set of fingerprints, that reveals in gory detail every aspect of the applicant's private life. These details are then scrutinized to determine whether the applicant is morally fit to become a member of the Florida Bar, a "voluntary" organization that all lawyers are forced to join to practice law in the courts of Florida.

The idea of having an organized bar association to which all practicing lawyers must belong is to make certain that those who dispense legal advice are adequately trained to do so and that all attorneys exude the highest degree of integrity. At odds with these efforts is the perception in the minds of many people that, generally speaking, attorneys are either incompetents who speak total gibberish or thieves.

In the olden days there were no bar associations or morality squads to regulate attorneys. An unwritten code of honor in a distinguished profession made such devices unnecessary. But in the modern world of cynicism and self-aggrandizement, lawyers and other professionals have their own private bureaucracies that tell them what is ethical, and who isn't.

These private bureaucracies have failed miserably in their purported missions of ensuring competency and guarding against lapses of ethics. Malpractice is rampant, and instances abound of unscrupulous professionals preying upon the public. To make matters worse, some of the regulations imposed by organized bar associations, the very people who are supposed to oversee those who uphold the law, have been declared illegal and unconstitutional.

Now, the gatekeepers into the legal profession had found sufficient cause to investigate Earl's fitness to join their ranks. The section of his application on litigation in which he had been involved read like a rap sheet to the members of the committee appointed to judge his moral fitness to be a lawyer, and so he had been summoned to a meeting room of the motel to answer for these sins. *How ironic,* he thought to himself, *that actions I had taken as a matter of principle placed my morality as a potential attorney in doubt.*

The investigation delayed Earl's admission to the bar. He felt a peculiar sense of déjà vu when he attended the swearing-in ceremony at the court of appeals where Marilyn and a number of other young people became lawyers. Fortunately, no one asked him why he couldn't join them, sparing him the embarrassment of trying to explain what was happening to him.

The delay in his admission also put him in a difficult position as he hunted down attorney jobs in Miami. He moved there even though Marilyn explained apologetically that she couldn't stay with him. She had found a place of her own, and her parents would have a fit if she started living with a man. But Earl had a plan. He tracked down Wade Wilson, an old college roommate of his who he knew was living in the Miami area. Earl and Wade had a blood pact where Earl swore that someday he would pull Wade out of the comforts of his home to live off the land in the rugged mountains, away from civilization.

When he finally found Wade, Earl appeared at his doorstep. "I have come for you," he said with mock gravity.

After a few rounds of bear hugs and shots of Jack Daniels, Wade agreed to put Earl up for a while until he got settled. A few days later, Frank managed to get him a part-time position as a law clerk at his firm until he could get admitted to the bar. A few weeks later, he received the notice to appear before the Board of Bar Examiners at the Orlando Marriott.

Marilyn insisted on driving up to Orlando with Earl for his appointment with the "Thought

Police." They pulled into the parking lot just fifteen minutes before his scheduled appearance, bleary-eyed after the long, early morning ride to Orlando. They walked into the lobby where Marilyn sat down wearily as Earl tracked down an official from the board who told him to wait in the lobby. He got a paper for Marilyn and sat next to her, waiting nervously.

A young woman approached him in the lobby. "Earl Warren?"

He looked at Marilyn briefly before following the young woman upstairs to the conference room where the interrogation would take place. He sat down next to a stenographer who was sitting alone on one side of the tables that had been arranged in a large square in the middle of the room.

An array of people sat along the three remaining sides of the square, looking down at their papers and whispering to one another.

An older man at the center of the table directly across from Earl called the meeting to order. "Our first applicant for today is Mr. Earl Warren. No relation to the former chief justice, I trust?" He smiled at his own joke. No one laughed. "Mr. Warren," he continued, "the members of the board are concerned about some of the items on your application. At this time I would like to turn the floor over to Mr. Rubin, our attorney, for a few questions."

"Yes, Mr. Warren," Rubin began, standing from his chair, as he eyed a paper held in his hand. "Why did you file this lawsuit against the university?"

"The students voted for an independent radio station, and the university refused because they wanted to censor the broadcasts. This was a clear violation of the First Amendment, but the students couldn't hire a lawyer. So I filed the lawsuit on my own behalf to rectify the situation."

"You sued the school?"

"Yes, sir."

"And when you lost, you asked the Supreme Court to hear your case; is that right?"

"I didn't exactly lose. The trial judge wouldn't grant an injunction, but he wouldn't sign an order denying it either. So I had no other avenue of relief. Technically, under the statute the Supreme Court had jurisdiction to hear the case, but they denied cert. Now that I have graduated, the case has become moot, so I voluntarily dismissed it."

A man to Earl's left decided to ask a question.

"Mr. Warren, Chief Justice Moorehead of the Supreme Court has given many speeches expressing concern over the proliferation of litigation and the crisis faced by the courts in trying to deal with ever-increasing caseloads. Don't you think the courts can do without some of these cases you have been pursuing?"

Earl paused for a minute before answering.

"I had the misfortune of watching as my colleagues were admitted to the bar, unable to join with them because of this inquiry. But as I watched, I noticed that the oath that each was asked to take states that an attorney is duty bound to uphold the Constitution of the United States. There may be no greater right under that constitution than the freedom to speak. To watch an institution of higher learning deprive young people of that right was so outrageous that I felt compelled to act.

"I may have made mistakes in the way I pursued the case but was placed into the position of representing myself because of the actions of the university. But in any event the suit itself was based on the highest of ideals. I know Justice Moorehead is concerned about too much litigation, but I'm sure he would never deprive a person of the right to seek redress in a court of law for a wrong that has been committed.

"Incidentally, I would like to point out that the university filed a motion arguing that the whole matter was frivolous. That motion was denied by the Court. I'm sure that if the chief justice and the other members of the Court thought otherwise, they wouldn't have done that."

After another pause, Rubin continued his interrogation.

"Have the criminal charges filed against you for the unlawful possession of alcoholic beverages been resolved yet?" he asked in an accusatory tone. Earl was puzzled.

"As indicated in my application, those charges were dropped by the State after I filed a brief showing that the ordinance under which I was charged is unconstitutional."

Rubin seemed perplexed. He had difficulty accepting the idea that such a law was unconstitutional. He was the type of person who believed the State could do no wrong. He also couldn't believe that Earl had actually prevailed in one of these courthouse misadventures.

"What about this speeding ticket. Have you paid that fine yet?" he asked.

"That's on my application also. I filed an appeal from that fine which is currently pending. I obtained a court order that stayed the fine pending appeal."

Rubin was somewhat irritated by these responses. Earl wondered if he was supposed to be more apologetic about asserting his rights in court. He didn't think of himself as litigious. Except for the suit against the university, he didn't initiate any of this litigation. Once he was dragged into court by the government, he had no reason to apologize for fighting back.

After what seemed like hours of interrogation, Rubin suddenly ended the questioning in exasperation. The chairman thanked Earl politely and excused him from the room.

As he closed the door, he heard someone in the conference room after a momentary pause let out a long "sheeeeesh."

Earl walked down the stairs to the lobby, feeling relieved.

He was certain they would let him into the bar. During the time he was in that room, the members of the committee stared at him intently, as if trying to detect some nervous twitch or other sign that he was not fully possessed of a complete deck of playing cards. Although not the typical would-be attorney in awe of the power of the committee, he was polite and quite lucid.

Marilyn bolted up from her chair and hurried over to meet him midway through the lobby, an anxious expression on her face.

"Well? How'd it go?"

"It went very well, Marilyn. I think I'm in." He gave her a hug and a smile that reassured her. They turned and started walking out of the hotel. "They just wanted to look me over to see if I had two heads or something. They wouldn't dare to keep a fine person such as myself out of the profession."

"Right, they probably think you'd sue them if they didn't let you in," she said with a laugh. "They'd be right," Earl said in a serious tone.

Marilyn stopped suddenly and searched Earl's eyes in alarm. He looked at her for a split second before his face broke out into a broad grin. He started to laugh as he took her by the arm and walked to her car.

"Come on, let's get outta here. I'm starting to not like Orlando."

CHAPTER XIII
RAISING THE ANTE

A year had passed since Earl received the notice from the Florida Board of Bar Examiners that he had passed their inspection of his morality and could become a member of the Florida Bar.

When he received the notice, a quiet calm spread throughout Earl's mind and body. *At last I have completed my penance for my activities in law school*, he thought to himself at the time. Eschewing the pomp and circumstance of a mass swearing-in ceremony scheduled for weeks later, he talked the appeals court judge for whom Marilyn clerked into giving him the oath in the judge's chambers.

Once he became a real lawyer, Earl was officially designated "of counsel" to Frank's firm. That meant that although he was not an employee, he worked on cases that were given to him by the firm. He was also free to take his own cases. The cases from the firm were assigned to him by Albert, a young attorney who, on paper at least, was the head of the firm. In actuality, Pete, a gruff older man, was in charge. Pete was not a lawyer, but he made all of the major decisions. He was the office manager and ran the small practice with an iron fist.

Albert and Pete had a strange relationship. They lived together and worked together. They shared the large main office where Albert met clients and collected his fees, usually in cash. Albert would sit and confer with his clients while Pete tapped away at his computer.

Usually, Pete was working on his own case even though Albert was listed as his attorney. He spent most of the day working on a document that he would print out for Albert's signature.

Albert and Pete would discuss legal concepts or strategy in the case. Occasionally, these conversations would begin to get heated. Earl and the others in the office would hear Albert in a whining tone dispute some point being made by Pete. Then Pete could be seen closing the door, an odd smile on his face. In a few minutes the whole office cringed as shouts from Albert and the loud bellowing voice of Pete could be heard coming from the inner sanctum. Then there would be silence. Eventually they would emerge, chatting casually as if nothing had happened.

Albert and Pete saw themselves as soldiers in the battle against the forces of injustice and regression in the world. Though their relationship was strange, Earl could appreciate their sentiments and felt oddly at home in their firm. Pete's case was a civil rights lawsuit against the county. The county wanted to bulldoze his property in retaliation for the nasty letters he had written to the zoning department. The dispute had escalated into a federal case – literally – which when stacked on the floor was at least 3 feet high.

The suit was not the case of the century, but Earl was more than happy to assist when asked by "the boys," as the two were affectionately called by the others in the office. Working on the case was welcome relief from the tedious uncontested divorces to which Earl was usually assigned.

Although crusaders against the forces of evil, the boys knew that they had to make a living on cases that had nothing to do with the rights of the individual or righting some terrible wrong.

They set up their fledgling law practice in a small suite of offices on Biscayne Boulevard just on the northern outskirts of the city. They had chosen this area of Miami because the office was located around the corner from the Immigration and Naturalization Service. Albert paid his bills primarily by handling immigration cases, a field of law near the bottom in the legal pecking order.

Before he was admitted Earl spent a lot of time filling out endless forms and accompanying aliens to be interviewed for permanent residency status which, in the parlance of the trade, meant that he helped them to get their "green card," the coveted proof of legal status in America.

Because of the location of the office, rent was at rock bottom prices. Even though Biscayne Boulevard, a state and federal highway, was the grand gateway into the magic city, the area along the boulevard had been allowed to deteriorate for years. Earl could greet the sleazy prostitutes that walked the boulevard on his way into the office, watch the sleeping people on bus benches, or the homeless who panhandled on either side of the street for their daily fix of crack, which was bought, sold, or bartered for sex at the many crack houses that could be found just a block or two away from anywhere along the boulevard. Earl often thought this unofficial "red light district" gave visitors an honest welcome to Miami along its main thoroughfare.

When Earl first arrived, he was greeted by the shocking content of the local evening news, complemented in the surreal fashion of Miami with light stories on visits by the Girl Scouts to lonely retirees on Miami Beach. One of the first stories Earl remembered hearing on the news was when a man, stark naked and covered in blood, approached a police officer *carrying the head of his girlfriend*, who he had apparently believed had been possessed by the devil.

This story was, of course, followed later by a story about a student at a local high school that won the spelling bee.

By now Earl had made the adjustment from the small college town to what many Miamians lovingly refer to as "Dodge City." Every once in a while something so bizarre would happen that he would wonder why he stayed. One night he was riding with Marilyn on State Road 836 to one of Miami's many nightclubs. 836 is a busy, multiple-lane highway. She suddenly came to a screeching halt in the middle of the highway. Earl was alarmed.

Any minute another car will come crashing into us, he thought to himself. "What are you doing?" he asked in a panic.

"What's that?" she asked, nodding towards the front of the car.

Earl was looking out the back of the car for the onrush of speeding headlights to descend upon them. He turned around and saw for the first time that there was the body of a black man lying less than twenty feet in front of them, illuminated by her headlights. He had apparently been thrown out of a car, as they could see red patches of pockmarks on his lifeless body where skin and flesh had been violently gouged from his torso and legs, probably from being smashed against the railing and the cars speeding by at 60 to 80 miles per hour.

Earl gulped. They exchanged glances at each other. There was no need to explain the look of surprise and horror on each other's faces. By that time, the highway patrol was already beginning to block the area off with their cruisers, blue lights flickering.

A trooper was waving them to go around.

In the midst of this carnage and chaos, Earl was learning his craft. The perverse mixture of human tragedy and almost comical flights of fancy on the part of Miami's denizens had seeped into the Dade County Courthouse, often the stage upon which events from the sublime to the ridiculous played themselves out. Earl's very first court hearing as a lawyer was a case in point.

He ushered Albert's immigrant client and a witness into the chambers of Judge Wilhelm Barron for a routine uncontested divorce. Barron was a short, rotund man with beady eyes and no neck to speak of. He spoke in a thick, European accent that sounded Austrian or Hungarian. He claimed to be a survivor of a Nazi labor camp, but there were rumors at the courthouse that questioned which side he was really on during the war.

"Vell, Counselor. Vat do we haff today?" he said as they sat at the table in front of his desk.

He was eyeing the young, dark-skinned man from Colombia there for his divorce.

"Just a simple uncontested divorce, your Honor," Earl replied as he opened his file and pulled out some papers.

"And vat is this young man's immigration status, counsel?"

"He is here on a visitor's visa, Your Honor, his application for permanent residence status is pending. But we are just here for –"

"I know vy you are here. But, unfortunately, I cannot grant dis divorce," the judge said, tossing the file at Earl. "He is not a resident, and he cannot get a divorce."

Earl was flabbergasted. "But, Your Honor–"

"I haff ruled, young man. Tell my secretary to send in ze next case on your way out." When Earl explained to Albert what happened, he was outraged.

The law was clear that an alien who had not yet been granted permanent residence was entitled to seek a divorce. There was a case directly on point. Albert decided to go down himself and confront Judge Barron. But the judge wouldn't budge. He didn't care about Albert's case. No alien would get a divorce in his court unless they had a green card, a rule that apparently was only applied to Hispanic-looking clients, or those who were obviously from Haiti.

He did not ask every client for their green card when they came in his chambers. Albert was miffed when he returned from the hearing.

"Well, what will you do?" Earl asked. Albert's client obviously couldn't afford an appeal.

"Just set it at one of the branch courts," Albert said casually as he flipped the file on Earl's desk. The branch courts were scattered throughout the sprawling county to accommodate people in outlying areas. These courts could hear uncontested divorces assigned to other judges downtown.

Earl did as he was told. The divorce was granted without incident a few weeks later.

Earl had just returned from another trip to the courthouse to end another marriage. His client, a young girl originally from Cuba, asked him to pose with her at the courthouse while her friend took their picture. She was like a tourist for a visit to the museum-like courthouse, or maybe she wanted to maintain uniformity to her scrapbook. After all, she had pictures of her wedding and the reception. Why not pictures of her divorce?

Earl plopped down in his chair and let the file land on the desk with a thud. Wilma, the young secretary, paged him. He had a call on line one.

"Hello?"

"Hi, Earl."

"Hi, Marilyn. How are the wheels of justice turning down at your end? I just ended another unhappy relationship myself."

"Another uncontested divorce?"

"Yeah. It's not very exciting, but I guess being a lawyer is not that glamorous after all."

"I know what you mean. Well, I called to invite you to a party. Remember Mark from law review?"

"How could I forget?"

"He's having a get-together with some other people from our law school. Sort of a mini class reunion."

"I'd love to."

"Great. I'll pick you up at 8:30. Bye."

"See you then."

Tonight would be another installment of what had turned into a long, awkward courtship between Earl and Marilyn. Marilyn was a very reserved, proper young woman whose caution and reluctance constantly kept them from becoming too intimate. By contrast, Earl seemed to live life on the edge, willing to take risks. He was not concerned about what others thought of him.

Earl was frustrated with the course their relationship was taking – or not taking. Every time they were in a position to get really romantic, something seemed to intervene, or Marilyn would suddenly stop herself and say goodnight. Marilyn was cautious. Too cautious, Earl thought, but she was very tolerant when Earl had found himself in these difficult situations, as with the radio station suit and when he was flunked out of environmental law.

Marilyn would be driving again tonight, of course. Earl's license had been suspended, the product of another one of his crusades from their law school days. He pulled open a drawer and took out the file, already getting thick with papers, from his license suspension case. He opened the file and looked through the papers again. They told the story about the chain of events that had lead him to where he was at the moment.

The paper notifying him of the suspension had come in an innocent-looking envelope from the Florida Department of Highway Safety and Motor Vehicles. His license had been suspended for failure to pay a traffic fine originating in Buford County. He had been directed to contact the court there to resolve the problem. When he read the words "Buford County," he knew that something had gone wrong with the appeal he had filed from the speeding ticket he got while in Marilyn's car.

The appeal had been sitting in the Buford Circuit Court for two-and-a-half years by the time he received the notice that his license had been suspended. Just the month before, he thought that he should write to the Court and give them his new address but decided not to write. He thought the case may have been lost in the shuffle. If he were to write now, his letter would probably call attention to the case. *Better to let sleeping dogs lie,* he thought to himself. Besides, his mail was still being forwarded from his old address. He would be notified if something happened in the case.

Earl picked up the letter he had written to the traffic court about his case and the response he had received. A clerk wrote back explaining that the decision of the traffic judge had been affirmed. The order of the circuit judge who affirmed the decision of Judge Akins had been sent to Earl's old address, along with a form that gave Earl 10 days to pay the fine of $100, plus administrative expenses, failing which his license would be suspended. The clerk had sent Earl a copy of the order, the notice, and the envelope in which she had originally sent the papers. The envelope had a postal notice that said "Moved – Forwarding Order Expired" stamped on the front.

At first Earl blamed himself for not notifying the court of his address. Then he began to wonder why he *did* receive the notice that his license was suspended. Looking through the papers he had been sent by the clerk, he saw that a second notice was sent to his old address informing him that his license was being suspended and giving a form printed by the Department of Motor Vehicles that he had to sign and return, with his payment, in order to reinstate his license. These papers had been sent to his old address even though the form had his name and correct Miami address printed on the front. *How sneaky,* he thought to himself.

By sending this notice to the wrong address, not only was his "driving privilege" suspended, but he was also unaware that Judge Akins' ruling had been affirmed by the "appeals court," which was really just another judge who sat in another part of the same ultramodern courthouse of the cow pastures. The 30-day deadline to appeal the second judge's decision had already passed by the time Earl was notified that his license was suspended. Surely the clerk knew that he would not receive the second notice, since the first had already been returned. This gave the impression that the clerk purposefully sent the paper to the wrong address to avoid any further appeals.

Earl admitted to himself that he was wrong not to notify the court of his address. But the case had been just sitting there for more than two years. After pondering the complexities of Earl's existential issues of traffic law, there came a one word conclusion "affirmed."

One might expect parties to such a case to begin to grow old, maybe change their whereabouts. What would the clerk have done for a case that had been discovered after ten years without a ruling? Would she have expected that maybe the person involved might have forgotten about the whole thing, or did she believe that they had been rushing to their mailbox every day, anxious for the words of wisdom so long in coming?

Might she not make some effort to locate the long lost traffic offender instead of sending repeated notices to the same address from which her earlier correspondence had been returned?

Earl began to imagine in his mind what was taking place at the Buford County Clerk's Office. He concocted a vision of the clerks gleefully stamping papers and typing up forms as they passed around office gossip. Their only respite from the daily drudgery was to think up imaginative ways to drive the public crazy. On the wall is a picture of the "Clerk of the Month," who just discovered yet another absurd catch-22 to add to the already formidable arsenal they had accumulated over the years. Taped to the wall is a copy of a recent letter sent out by a clerk:

"Dear Death Row Inmate:

We are sorry, but even though you are innocent, your attorney did not file your papers in triplicate. The execution will have to proceed as scheduled."

A court of law is not supposed to be a bureaucracy. People who have been dragged into court, even traffic court, deserve fair treatment. The letters Earl received from the clerk's office had brought back all the anger and frustration he remembered feeling after his humiliation by Judge Akins. He had allowed himself to think that the injustice that had been done to him would be corrected in due course. But his appeal had been cast aside with a cryptic one-word disposition.

There was no explanation, no reasoning, and no further appeal.

Then Earl decided to do some research. He found cases that allowed an appeal to be filed past the due date if, through the actions of a clerk, the party was wrongfully deprived of the right to pursue the appeal. He had prepared a petition asking the court of appeals that presided over the Court of Cow Pastures to hear the case. Earl pulled out the order from the appeals court directing the State of Florida to "show cause" why the petition should not be granted.

The order meant that the petition showed a preliminary basis for relief.

Earl leaned back in his chair as he thought about his giddy – and naive – reaction to that order. At last he would get fair consideration of the case. At the least the court would send the case back for a reconsideration as to the amount of the fine. Maybe the court would write a lengthy opinion that would make the Buford judges hesitate about turning their courtrooms into a poker game where the loser paid "double or nothing."

But before Earl had even sent his reply to the brief filed by the government, the court had already dismissed the case. Earl reached for his rulebook as he put down the order he had received from the court. He checked the rules again to be sure that he was right. He was. The court ruled before the time had expired for him to file a reply. He had filed a motion for rehearing of the court's order, quoting the rules and pointing out that the court had violated them.

This motion touched off another paper tug-of-war between the clerk's office and the court on one side, and Earl on the other.

Instead of ruling on the motion, the court ordered that the motion be stricken as untimely.

But under the rules the motion appeared to be filed within the time limits. Earl sent a letter of complaint to the clerk. The clerk responded that the rules had been interpreted to mean something other than what they said.

Earl sent another letter of complaint. He pleaded with the clerk. All he wanted was a court to take a serious look at the case. The clerk responded indignantly that he was merely doing the bidding of the court, and if Earl wanted to pursue the matter further, he should file a motion with the court. Earl filed a paper asking the court to grant a rehearing on its own motion, citing a case that allowed such a procedure even when a motion for rehearing was untimely.

Earl shook his head as he read the response of the attorney for the government to this paper. Then he searched back through the papers that he had filed up to that date. None of the letters or papers indicated that he had become an attorney while the case had been on appeal. He was not quite sure why he didn't reveal that he was an attorney in this case. The merits of the case shouldn't depend on whether the person arguing the case is an attorney. Maybe he wanted to test this theory in practice. Maybe his experience in the radio station case still haunted him.

Had he been an attorney, he may have fared better. He sensed that he was being humored by the court of appeals, but that there was no chance he would win the case.

He also wasn't sure why he decided to write "Esquire" after his name when he filed that last motion. Maybe he thought the court would listen, now that they knew he was legit. Whatever the reason, the revelation made the attorney for the government react as if she was shot out of a cannon. She filed a paper in the court that demeaned Earl as a person and a lawyer. She ridiculed him as a lunatic who as a law student lost a traffic case and as an attorney was taking up her precious time with a "frivolous" appeal. She urged the Court to read the nasty letters Earl had sent to the clerk and to impose a fine against him for using his law school training to file whatever he wanted without regard for the law or the court.

Earl wasn't sure why this case had so offended her. Maybe she was the dumping ground for pro-se papers in the office and resented such a low station in life. This case did not take up so much of her precious time. All she had to do was sit back and watch as the court and the clerk dismantled the case without her having to do a thing. She was in no mood to be forgiving or to be tolerant of another person who acted on what he believed to be principle, even if the principle was, to her, flawed. Maybe the stakes were too low to justify the time she spent to pay attention, even for just a few minutes, to the many pro se litigants whose cases were argued and inevitably lost.

Whatever deep-seated resentment had been unleashed, the paper filed by the prosecutor had the desired effect, even though the paper was little more than pure character assassination with no legal support. Within days of receiving the paper, Earl signed for an envelope bearing the return address for the court of appeals that had been sent by certified mail.

He knew before opening the envelope that he was in trouble. Usually documents are sent certified as a means of intimidating the recipient. Inside the envelope was an order from the Court telling him to show cause why he shouldn't be fined as requested.

Earl had responded to the order with a lengthy brief filled with citations showing that the Court could not impose a fine under the law. By sending the order to show cause, the Court had already ruled that the case had arguable merit. The law was clear that the Court could not punish a litigant just for losing a case. Such a punishment could only be justified if the position of that person had no arguable merit.

When Earl had written the brief, he knew that he was wasting his time. This case was not about a speeding ticket or the legality of the way in which the Buford County Court was run. The case was about *power*. A fundamental precept of the constitutional order is that America is a nation of laws, not of men (or nowadays women, too). The rule of law was intended to prevent the unbridled exercise of raw power because those who wrote the Constitution knew that power corrupts the mind of the person who is granted the right to wield it.

In the delicate system of checks and balances devised by the creators of the constitutional system, the courts of the country are charged with the responsibility of applying the law in a given case dispassionately and equally to all that come before the court. The crowd and popular will may cry for the bowed head of the accused. But the law protects those who have been accused (and who are not guilty) or provides comfort to those who have been wronged. The law is like a machine that produces the same result under the same circumstances with certainty regardless of popular whim or the clouded judgment born of the heat of the moment.

But the central cog in the machinery of the law is the judge who must interpret and apply that law dispassionately even while human emotions make that judge recoil at the repugnance of the accused or feel anger towards the young man who dares to defy authority. In the courtroom a judge can easily succumb to the temptation to let his emotions decide the outcome, rationalizing the result afterward.

Earl had become that young man sticking his middle finger high in the air in the direction of the bench, even though such a gesture is a form of speech supposedly protected by the First Amendment. An outraged judge would be expected to throw such a young man in chains and to be quickly affirmed by his colleagues on appeal. To maintain order, to maintain *power*, the judges have given themselves the right to give vent to their fury against any person who dares to question their judgment or to trivialize their power by seeking answers to questions of no importance to them.

So when the order had come from the court of appeals, the last paper in Earl's file, he was not surprised. The Court had fined him for arguing as he had in the case. *Fined him for his ideas.*

Now he had to decide what to do next, if anything.

Earl looked again at the order before putting it back in the file with the stack of other papers. The significance of the amount of the fine had not been lost on him. He was fined $100.

The fine for his speeding ticket had been doubled again.

CHAPTER XIV
PRISONER OF CONSCIENCE

Marilyn arrived promptly, as usual, to pick up Earl at his small apartment on Miami Beach.

They were headed for an affluent section of Coral Gables, a Mediterranean style city that is one of the many municipalities that is part of the Miami megalopolis, for the "reunion" party at Mark's house. Earl was preoccupied with thoughts of their relationship. They stopped at a draw bridge that had gone up to let a boat full of revelers pass through and out into the dark ocean.

"Marilyn, we are very different, aren't we?"

"What do you mean?"

"You are a very upstanding citizen. Very *proper*. You come from a nice family. You're very conservative. I'm sort of brash and unpredictable.

Here we are sitting in this car, and I can't drive because of another one of my principles."

She looked at him, realizing for the first time that he had embarked upon a serious conversation. "What are you trying to say, Earl?" she asked with a look of some concern.

"I'm just wondering why a nice person such as you would want to hang around with a guy like me, that's all." He looked down at his hands.

She laughed and squeezed one of them. "That's what my mother keeps asking me."

The draw bridge had gone down, and she had put the car in gear, waiting for traffic to start. "I know we're different, Earl. I don't know why I like you. I just do. Why do you like me? I'm too stuffy and no fun, right?"

He looked up at her and smiled. She returned his smile as they started over the bridge.

Maybe they balanced each other out. He gave her a sense of adventure; she kept him from going over a cliff. But he didn't analyze the situation. He just knew how he felt about her.

"Well, I don't know, Marilyn. You can get pretty crazy yourself sometimes, you know."

When they pulled into Mark's spacious two-story home, Earl realized that Mark had done very well for himself. He was working for one of the big firms in town, obviously making plenty of money. His girlfriend with whom he shared the house was an attorney with her own small firm.

Their combined incomes provided them with a very comfortable lifestyle. Along the street and in the driveway were the Porsches, BMWs, and a Mercedes, parked like signposts marking another gathering of young people with money.

Earl and Marilyn were greeted at the door by Sherryl, Mark's "significant other." She and Marilyn pecked at each other's cheeks briefly, missing by a good two inches. Sherryl smiled at Earl and beckoned them into the house with a sweep of her arm. The party was well underway, jazz music playing just loud enough to be heard, but not too loud to drown out the conversation of the small crowd of people in the living room. The room was filled with the typical hum created by the sum total of the crosscurrents of communication flowing in the clumps of small groups assembled within the press of humanity, their combined force animated by the energy of each being part of a single contrived event commonly referred to as a "party."

A petite, pretty young woman with elfin features approached Marilyn. They kissed each other lightly, this time on the mark.

"Earl, this is Debbie Gelber, Huey's beau." Earl had met Huey, who worked as an attorney with the Florida Bar, a few months earlier. "Debbie, this is Earl Warren," Marilyn said.

"No relation to *the* Earl Warren, unfortunately," Earl replied, smiling. Debbie looked at him with a blank expression. She apparently didn't know what he meant.

"Another lawyer, I suppose?" she said in a friendly tone.

"I hope you don't talk too much lawyer talk," she said, turning to Marilyn. "It gets to be very boring."

"What do you expect with all these lawyers in one room, Debbie? But I know what you mean," Marilyn said.

"What kind of lawyer are you, Earl?" Debbie asked politely. "A boring one, I'm afraid," he replied. This time she laughed. Sherryl rejoined their group.

"I see you're making yourselves at home," she said, glancing around the room to make sure everyone was having a good time. The house was filled with young, upwardly mobile professionals dressed fashionably and holding their wine glasses or drinks, chatting amiably and sampling pate'. One of the waiters hired for the occasion walked up to Earl.

"Can I get you something?"

Yes, outta here, Earl thought to himself. "Two white wines, if you don't mind," Earl replied with a weak smile and slight nod of the head.

"So Earl, Marilyn tells me that you have your own practice. Where are your offices?" asked Sherryl, turning slightly in his direction.

"Biscayne and 79th Street. The low rent district. Yours?"

"Our offices are on Brickell Avenue." Brickell Avenue is the financial center of Miami, a pleasant, tree-lined street with impressively designed glass skyscrapers on either side filled with offices overlooking the water and downtown Miami. Only the elite could afford offices on Brickell. As they were comparing offices, Mark had joined them, shaking Earl's hand.

"Hi, Earl. Been making any waves lately? Earl has his own practice you know, honey," he said to Sherryl before Earl had a chance to answer.

"I know," she said with a smile and glint in her eye. "Any interesting cases, Earl?" Mark asked.

"Lately things have become very chaotic. With the change in governments in Haiti, the Haitian refugees are going to have a harder time with their political asylum cases. Why just this week a judge at the Krome Avenue Detention Camp was talking about how the Ton Ton Macoutes were being attacked by the citizens over there. The judge actually said that a Macoute would probably have a good claim to asylum. After all these years of denying asylum applications of Haitians who have been terrorized by the Macoutes saying it was isolated incidents or just a figment of their imaginations, now they are going to grant asylum to those bastards just because they helped keep the dictator we supported in power all these years.

"Can you believe that?" Earl looked at Debbie. She had a glazed look in her eyes. She looked at Marilyn, dumbfounded.

"Excuse me," Sherryl said as she headed into the crowd to attend to one of her guests.

"I think I'll head for the bar," Debbie said, glancing at Marilyn and giving Earl a weak smile. "I'll join you. I need a refill," Marilyn said, giving Earl a wink and blowing him a kiss.

Mark watched their reaction, apparently amused. "Boy, you sure know how to clear a room," said Mark.

"I guess I can't count on them for next week's animal liberation rally, huh?" Earl said, shaking his head.

Mark laughed. "What do you mean? You don't see anyone here wearing fur coats, do you?"

"Yeah, right. Next time try turning the air conditioning up a few notches and see if that holds true. This is Florida, you know."

"Ah, I see you haven't changed since law school," Mark said, draining his glass. "I think I'll join the lovely ladies at the bar," he said as he began to move in that direction.

"Hey, Earl the Pearl!" Earl heard the voice of Huey, who nearly caused him to spill his drink with his forceful slap on the back. "Howya' doin'?"

"Hi, Huey." Huey was a dark-haired young man who made friends very easily. He was a man's man. He was always looking for a partner to play tennis or putting together a basketball game or a few hours of touch football with the guys. Earl liked Huey, even though they were a stark contrast in personalities. Huey would never be caught taking life seriously. He had gained a position at the local office of the Florida Bar working for Pat Gelber, Debbie's father. Most of the times Earl called there for him, he was occupied on the tennis courts that were conveniently located on the same floor as the offices of the Florida Bar, on Brickell Avenue.

The Florida Bar was the Thought Police for people like Earl who had gotten past the Florida Board of Bar Examiners and had joined the ranks of attorneys. The bar was charged with the responsibility of enforcing "ethics" among the lawyers in the state. Huey was one of the attorneys who supposedly prosecuted errant lawyers. The Florida Bar had taken heat from a number of reform groups whose members had been burned by attorneys. They said most of the complaints were denied. They were right.

"Look, Earl, I have to talk to you about something. Pat is looking for another attorney. The job is yours if you want it."

"Are you kidding?"

"No, really," Huey continued. He hadn't detected the note of sarcasm in Earl's voice. "Don't worry, the work is very easy. Nine-to-five, no overtime. Last girl we hired, I had to walk into her office and talk to her. She was working too hard. I grabbed her file away from her. 'Why don't you go shopping?' I said. You'd make a fine addition to our staff, Earl. Besides which, we can spend more time working on our playbook for next season."

Earl was the wide receiver on the Florida Bar's football team. Huey was the quarterback. "Let me think about it, Huey," Earl said. He didn't feel like confronting him then about what he really thought of the Florida Bar. Besides which, he didn't want to give up some of the cases he had been working on the past year.

"Okay, just let me know. I'll see ya around." Huey headed in the direction of the bar as Earl scouted around the room for Marilyn. He spotted her laughing hysterically at one of Mark's jokes across the room. He decided to give her some space. She was enjoying herself, and he didn't want to spoil her good time just because he was miserable. The depth of the people gathered for this party was paper thin, and Earl resented having to pretend that he was a part of them.

He decided to join the mass exodus to the bar, where he exchanged his dainty glass of white wine for a cold, working-class bottle of beer, which he swigged with as much lack of grace as he could muster. As the night wore on, he spent his time chatting with the help when he wasn't standing or sitting with Marilyn, suppressing grimaces at the banal banter of Debbie or listening to the umpteenth lawyer talk about a case.

Young lawyers in particular tend to become obsessed with the details of the procedures and events in their cases that are so new to them. They plod endlessly forward, oblivious to the fact that their fascination is not shared by their listeners, including the ones who will soon recount their own boring tale of how their motion was so cleverly drafted but was denied by the dim-witted judge.

Earl excused himself from one of these narratives, not that the young man speaking in earnest to their group had noticed. He made his way to the bathroom as much for some peace and quiet as to heed the call of nature. He stopped in the middle of the hallway leading to the bathroom when he saw the door open and close, a young woman glancing at him with a guilty expression on her face as she brushed by him. He had noticed when she opened the door that a gathering of people were inside, one of them hunched over the basin. He could guess what they were doing.

He walked to the end of the hall to find another bathroom. Finding none, he turned to head back into the living room just as Huey emerged from the bathroom, his back to Earl. He saw Huey lift his hand to his nose and heard the air rushing into his nostrils in two short bursts as Huey bounded into the living room.

I think now is a good time to leave, Earl thought to himself as he emerged from the hallway, his mission thwarted. He walked over to Marilyn, who was talking with Debbie. She, at least, was having a good time. She also had had a few too many glasses of wine.

"Marilyn, my dear, may I have a word with you?" he said in her ear as he pulled her gently away. Debbie giggled and waved to them before disappearing into the thinning crowd of people.

"Earl, Mark invited us to go swimming."

"We didn't bring our bathing suits."

"We don't need them." Earl looked at her disapprovingly.

"Oh, come on, sweetheart. You wanted to get wild and crazy, didn't you? Now I'm ready."

She must really be drunk, he thought to himself. *She never calls me "sweetheart."*

"Okay, *darling*. And would you also like to join the party in the bathroom? They're snorting coke. It's a regular Hoover convention in there, including our illustrious representative from the Florida Bar Association."

"Really?" she seemed to sober slightly.

"Come on," he said as he escorted her to the door. "I can just see the headlines: 'Judge's Aide Busted at Yuppie Coke Party in Coral Gables.'" They saw Sherryl on the way to the front door. "Have to go now," Earl said without stopping. "I have to get home early and rest up. I have an indecent exposure trial on Monday to prepare for." He just barely caught a glimpse of her face as she opened her mouth to say something before the door closed.

He steadied Marilyn, walking her to the passenger side of her car. "You mind giving me your keys, baby doll? I don't relish digging them out of your purse. No telling what I might find in there."

"But you can't drive."

"*You're* the one that can't drive."

After a moment's hesitation, she fumbled in her purse for her keys. He let her in and waited as she plopped down into the passenger seat, her head rolling backward. He closed her door before climbing in himself and starting the car. They roared away from the house with a peal of spinning tires.

"Earl, you're such a stick-in-the-mud. But I love you anyway," she said, her eyes closed.

Earl looked at her, surprised. He wondered if she was just drunk or if she was revealing her true feelings for him. He pulled into traffic and headed down the road, trying to get his bearings so he could decide on the best route to Marilyn's place.

As he was passing through an intersection, Marilyn pointed to the left and asked him to pull into the gas station on the corner. Earl swung the car over and into the station. Within seconds, a police cruiser pulled in behind him, blue lights flashing.

"What's the problem, officer?" Earl asked. He was already out of the car, standing next to the open door on the driver's side of the gleaming Corvette. The officer, a young Cuban man with bulging biceps, approached him.

"Just give me your license and registration," said the officer without expression. Earl hesitated.

"I don't have it. I was just –"

The officer didn't wait for an explanation. He grabbed Earl and spun him around. "Hands on the car," he barked. Earl complied, stunned. Then he was handcuffed.

The officer pulled him forcefully to the back of the cruiser and pushed him into the back seat before getting in behind the wheel. He asked for Earl's name, which he put into his computer.

"You mind telling me why you arrested me?" Earl asked.

"You know your license is suspended?" he responded, ignoring the question. "I know; it's in court. But you arrested me before you knew that. Why?"

"You didn't see that no-left-turn sign? I was sitting right across from you, and you made an illegal turn right in front of me. You think I was just gonna sit there and do nothin'?"

"With all the crime in Miami, you're busting me for an illegal left turn? You can't do that, anyway. You're violating my civil rights," Earl blurted out. He couldn't believe the words were coming out of his mouth.

"I haven't laid a hand on you," said the officer as he turned to look back at Earl, "*yet*."

By this time Marilyn had come to the window. She pleaded for the officer to let Earl go. He wouldn't listen. She asked him if she could follow him to the stockade. A hard rain started to fall as she stood there.

"Suit yourself," said the officer.

With that, he put away his paperwork and screeched out of the parking lot of the gas station. He flew out into the street and onto the interstate at breakneck speed. The rain was coming down so hard Earl could barely see out the window. But the officer screamed down the highway. At one point he hit a huge puddle that engulfed his entire windshield, blocking his vision completely. Earl sat in the back seat, his hands cuffed behind his back.

He was terrified.

When they got to the stockade, the officer pulled Earl out of the cruiser. They both ran to the entrance in the downpour, the officer holding onto Earl's arm. Once inside, Earl was subjected to the humiliation of being booked into the county jail like a common criminal. He stood there, wet and shivering, as another officer took down his vital statistics. Then he was lead against a wall where mug shots were taken. His fingers were rolled on a pad and pressed onto a card. Then he was led into a barren concrete holding cell about 12 feet wide and 15 feet long.

Several other people were already there.

Another inmate was being held in an adjacent cell. He let out periodic screams in Spanish. They made an odd assortment of prisoners. Among the several sleazy types were a few members of the blue collar working class. Another younger man was dressed nicely but was falling-down drunk. Earl felt awkward and out of place but tried not to show it.

He sat silently as the other inmates made small talk. He knew if they found out he was a lawyer, he would be bombarded with questions.

Earl felt as if he were in a dream. He could not believe that he was sitting in jail. As time passed, he began to feel a creeping sense of intense restlessness. He wondered how much time had passed. He had to have been in there at least an hour but had no way of knowing.

He studied the stark walls and cracked concrete floor. The horror of confinement began to dawn on him for the first time. His restlessness had grown to a panic state, lying just below the surface. He wondered how much time would pass before he could no longer contain the panic and what would happen if he lost control.

Then he heard a metallic clanging sound echo in the chambers that had become his own private hell. A guard appeared at the front of their cage, opening the door. "Earl Warren," he said. Earl rose and followed the guard obediently down the hallway and through a door into the processing area. Marilyn rushed up to him and threw her arms around his neck.

"Oh, Earl, I'm so sorry. Let's get out of this place." She led him out into the night. The rain had stopped. "My car's over there," she said as they walked.

"Good. You drive." Earl managed a weak smile.

They pulled out of the parking lot and into traffic, heading for Marilyn's apartment.

"They kept telling me to go away, but I stayed, waiting. About every 10 minutes I went up to the front counter and asked again about you. I guess they got tired of it. After a while they just let you go. What a nightmare."

"You can't imagine how horrible it was. Now I know what some of my clients have gone through. I'll never forget it."

She pulled the car into her apartment building and up the ramp into the parking garage.

They made their way into the elevators and into her apartment. The apartment was neat and clean. Her floor-length windows looked out over the bay and a view of the lights of the city sparkling in the night. Marilyn sat him down on the couch as she went into the small kitchen.

"Can I get you something to drink? I have some bourbon I keep for my dad."

"That sounds great."

"What do you drink it with?"

"You don't. Just pour some in a glass."

She handed him the glass and watched as he tossed the bourbon back in one swift motion. "I think I'll just bring the bottle into the living room," she said as she went back into the kitchen, bringing the bottle back and setting it down on the table in front of Earl. He poured another shot which he tossed down again, setting his empty glass on the table. He felt the usual warm feeling rising up from his stomach.

"I don't know how to thank you, Marilyn," he said, looking up at her. "You waited for me all that time in that, that hellhole." He felt his eyes well up with tears. He tried to fight the feelings surging up from deep inside. Marilyn slid on the couch next to him, putting her arm around him.

"No, no. It was all my fault. I had to get drunk at that stupid party. If you hadn't driven, we probably would be much worse off right now."

He was acutely aware that she used the term "we," which made him feel good for reasons he could not quite pinpoint.

She was gazing deeply into his eyes.

Earl met her gaze. His feelings of anguish were being overtaken by the impulse to take her in his arms. He did. Their lips met before he knew what was happening.

The mixture of the bourbon and his traumatic experience made him abandon all restraint.

He let his emotions carry him forward, pressing his lips hard against hers as he held her tight.

She grabbed him as the weight of his body pushed her backwards on the couch. Then she ran her hand down his back and across his buttocks, squeezing gently.

Earl pulled away from her for a moment, studying her face, his own showing a questioning look. She looked at him sweetly as she slowly unbuttoned her blouse, which she pulled apart to reveal her breasts, harnessed tightly by a black lace brassiere. Earl's mouth fell open ever so slightly as she reached behind her back with both hands and unleashed her breasts, which swayed from side to side as she cast her bra to the side. Earl cupped the mounds of soft flesh in his hands and leaned forward, burying his face again into hers.

Their bodies fell back onto the couch in slow motion. Earl hungrily kissed her lips and then her neck, slowly making his way down to her magnificent, firm breasts, the nipples protruding and hard. He flicked his tongue across her skin, caressing the sides of her torso gently with his hands.

Her eyes were closed, her face glowing with ecstasy. He pulled down her skirt and looked up for a moment. He searched her expression for approval as his hand slid upwards on the inside of her thigh.

Her eyes closed, and her head fell back onto the couch. Her lips parted in a faint smile.

She gasped when he entered her and then pursed her lips as their bodies fell into the rhythmic movement of love-making. Earl glanced down the side of her body, watching her breasts squeezed flat under his weight and her smooth legs arched up and around his own.

They both grimaced in delight, holding their breaths at the instant of the release that they shared together. Then Earl felt his body go limp. Marilyn was kissing his face, running her hands through his hair, smiling warmly at him.

At long last they had shared the moment of intimacy they had both wanted but were afraid to initiate. Now they could begin to share of each other with reckless abandon. They went into her bedroom. They showered together, washing each other's bodies.

Earl could not help the arousal he felt as he passed his hands over her body. She saw his erection and grabbed him with her hand, stroking him gently. Soon he had his hand thrust amidst the lather between her legs and they were clinging to each other again, furiously touching each other under the spray of the shower. He lifted her up and onto him, pressing her back against the wall of the shower. Afterward they let the water wash away the smell of their sex.

They made love again later in Marilyn's bed at a slower pace, taking the time to explore the curves and indentations of each other's bodies, and to learn how to give each other the most pleasure. Then Marilyn fell asleep. Earl decided to venture out onto the balcony and take in the breath-taking scene of the lights of Miami, the water glistening in the moonlight.

He sat looking out into the night. Images of Marilyn's supple body under his own were crowded out by unpleasant flashes of the holding area and the other inmates staring at him.

He turned his head in the direction of the sound of the sliding glass door opening. Marilyn came out, dressed in the old football jersey she wore around the apartment. She sat down on the floor next to him, hugging his leg. He put his hand on her head, smoothing her hair.

"We've had quite a night," he said absently.

"I'll say."

"I guess I should feel grateful to that cop for getting us together like this," he said quietly.

"That bastard," Marilyn growled. Earl was taken aback at how she had flared at the mention of his arrest.

"If only I had stopped being such an asshole and just paid the two dollars like everyone told me to, this never would have happened," Earl said.

"No, Earl. That's not you talking. You haven't done anything wrong. No one should be arrested just because they ask for a fair hearing of their case. You've paid a steep price for what you believe in, Earl. I hope you're not thinking of backing down now. That's not the same man I've cared for so much." She stood up and kissed him on the cheek. "I need some sleep, lover boy."

"You coming?"

"Not sure I can do that *again* – at least not right now," he said with an impish smile. As the door slid shut, Earl thought about what she had said.

He looked out from her balcony, scanning the skyline. The light of the sun that was soon to rise had already begun to seep into the air, gradually illuminating the city. Earl scanned the buildings, trying to pick out the Dade County Courthouse. In a few hours, the task would be made simple by the swarm of turkey buzzards that had developed the habit, appropriately enough, of circling overhead just above the top of the courthouse.

What crime had he committed that was deserving of the time he had spent in jail during the night that had just passed? What lesson was he to derive from his punishment? He had been so numb from the experience, and his night of love-making afterward, that he was just now feeling the outrage of the injustice that had been perpetrated against him.

From all indications he had been able to gather even during his short tenure as an attorney, he could see that the humiliation he had endured was part of a pattern in the courts which were growing more intolerant of ideas out of the mainstream of thought and less accessible to those who espoused such ideas. Now the gauntlet in this war over the future of the legal system of which Earl, as an officer of that very system of which he had now become a part, had been thrown down.

Would he become a silent accessory to the slow strangulation of honor and principle at the gateway to the only avenue for the weak and less powerful to seek justice, or would he stand up to be counted, and likely be knocked down, for the principles for which he had chosen to fight?

He knew the answer, and what he had to do.

CHAPTER XV
ROUND TWO

Ron Meyers instantly recognized the name on the court file he pulled down from the shelf for his next cert summary. He shuddered with the memory of the experience he had had with Earl Warren more than two years earlier. Much had changed in the years since that time, but the anger of the chief over the last episode with this crackpot had grown to legendary proportions.

He knew he wasn't likely to overlook this case.

Meyers noticed that the attorney for the state had ignored the deadline for responding to Earl's cert petition, and let out a low moan. That meant that the clerk's office had notified the chief who instructed the clerk to send out a notice to the attorney general's office of Florida to respond to the petition within 30 days. The chief had already been alerted to the case and was probably hoping the state would grill Earl, asking for sanctions he knew the chief would grant.

There would be no way to slip this one by the chief.

"Doesn't this guy have enough sense to stay as far away from here as he can?" he said aloud. This time Meyers had no intention of screwing around with the cert summary. If anything, he would write up the summary to favor Earl's side. He knew that his work would undergo intense scrutiny if this thing blew out of proportion.

As he read Earl's papers, he knew that all hope that this case would pass unnoticed was lost. Once the chief saw that this guy was asking them to review a traffic case, he knew there would be a small nuclear explosion upstairs. Meyers blew out a blast of air as he began to draft his memo. He recounted Earl's odd journey through the appellate courts. Again there was a question of jurisdiction, but a more subtle one. There was some doubt as to whether he had raised the issue he asked the Court to review early enough. When Meyers read the issue, he laughed out loud.

"You're crazy!" he shouted at his computer screen.

Earl argued that the extra $100 tacked onto his fine by the court of appeals was a violation of his constitutional rights. He bypassed the Florida Supreme Court for the same reason in the radio station case. There was no further appeal from the order of the court of appeals. He had filed a direct appeal from the order to the U.S. Supreme Court, asking them to declare the use of sanctions by an appeals court unconstitutional. He argued that the sanctions violated the right to petition the government for redress of grievances guaranteed in the First Amendment, his freedom of speech, and his access to the courts. He said that the fine was in retaliation for his criticism of the trial court and the court of appeals in his correspondence.

The state did not respond to the constitutional arguments. Instead, the attorney in Tallahassee assigned to the case had trivialized the whole affair. The thrust of his argument was that the Court had no jurisdiction. Meyers looked through the papers in the file again. There was no motion for sanctions. Meyers thought maybe the case might blow over, after all. The court wouldn't consider sanctions if no one asked.

But the cert summary went off like a string of firecrackers in the chambers of the justices.

Baker moaned when he saw the memo. He didn't know if he could save this guy from the wrath of the chief a second time. The court had become even more bold and reactionary in the years since the radio station case. This time the other justices might go along with the chief whom he knew would unleash his fury on this hapless Don Quixote.

In the chief's office a clerk put the stack of new cert summaries on the chief's desk and hurried out the door. He did not want to be around when the dam burst. The chief had been under siege lately and was in a foul mood. When a study by a group of students at Yale Law School came out saying that he ranked as one of the dumbest justices of all time, he became infuriated, then morose.

The past few years had not been kind to Moorehead. He felt fatigued and overburdened with the demands of his position. He no longer had the spark to lead the crusade of the conservative political philosophy that was taking charge at the Court. He was beginning to think seriously about letting Nathan Usery, a popular, intelligent justice who was fiercely loyal to the conservative cause, take the throne.

When he arrived in his chambers from the quiet lunch he had enjoyed with a senator, he sat down wearily behind his desk, looking at the mass of paperwork piled high. He started to sift through the pile of cert summaries without enthusiasm. Suddenly his eyes lit up. He pulled out the summary in Earl's case and scrutinized the paper.

As he read the summary, his face turned red and his nostrils flared.

The one legacy of his tenure on the Court was the crusade against pro se petitioners and useless litigation. He had successfully pushed through his plan to give greater power to judges to impose sanctions against litigants who pursued these claims in court and to encourage judges to use this new power. The plan was controversial. Studies showed that sanctions imposed by the waves of conservative judges appointed to the federal courts fell disproportionately on plaintiffs in general, and specifically on those that dared to assert violations of constitutional rights. To Moorehead, the studies only proved that the leftists were the ones jamming the courts with their activist causes that belonged in their bra-burning rallies, not the courts. The charge of judicial political retaliation was just sour grapes from the losing side of the clash between liberals and conservatives.

Earl's case was an effrontery: a direct slap in the face. Not only did he dare to come back to Moorehead's court with another hair-brained case, but now he was directly challenging the reform Moorehead had initiated. He was not about to let this punk get off so easily this time. Moorehead threw himself into the task of putting together a memo on the case.

The memo would be a brief expression of his views on the subject. He called these short memos "little snappers." He allowed all the rage he felt flow onto the pages.

When he had finished, he was spent. The task had been invigorating, and now he felt drained. He read over the memo and was satisfied. Then he sent it over to one of his most trusted law clerks. He was anxious for a reaction.

Moorehead's clerks gathered for a meeting about the memo. They had been concerned about the chief for some time. Aside from his bitterness he was starting to lose touch. They had tried to cover for him as much as possible. The memo he had written would further erode his credibility with the other justices. The language he used was simply inappropriate for a man in his position. But he was getting harder to reason with lately, and they knew he had a hard-on for Earl.

They decided to go into chambers as a group to have him reconsider sending out the memo, or at least tone down the language.

Moorehead was in a testy mood when the clerks piled into his chambers. When he realized what they wanted, he exploded.

"I will not have my credibility challenged by this, this PUNK!" He bellowed. "How dare he send a goddamn traffic case to my court! The majesty and importance of the cases we decide here are being ridiculed and sullied by this garbage." The clerks' eyes widened as the chief continued, raising his memo high in the air. "I will not change one word of this. In fact, this little snapper is now going to be an opinion."

The clerks looked at each other. "An opinion, sir?" one of them ventured to ask. "Here," the chief said, thrusting the cert summary at the clerk. "Take this and look at the court file. I want you to draft a summary of the case, and I want it on my desk by today. I will write the rest myself." He then curtly evicted them.

Justice Wade was mortified when he read the draft opinion sent to his chambers from the chief.

The chief had clearly gone way off the deep end this time. He was not only risking the ridicule he would surely bring on himself, but would likely damage the dignity of the Court itself if this opinion was ever published in the law books. Aside from the outrageous language he had used and the unseemly display of the chief venting his personal hatred of a litigant in a court opinion, what the chief proposed was ludicrous.

He was asking the other justices to join an opinion in a case he called frivolous. For that reason, they had to deny cert. But he wanted the court to issue an opinion on the denial of cert. In the many years that Wade had been on the Court, he could remember no case where the court had issued an opinion on the denial of cert.

On extremely rare occasions a single justice would write a *dissent* to denial of cert, vilifying his colleagues for not agreeing to consider an issue he thought demanded the attention of the Court. Such displays were an embarrassment to the Court and the other justices who wanted to maintain the mystique of the institution and recoiled at any hint that the justices lacked complete camaraderie.

Now the chief wanted the Court to refuse to hear the case on the merits but also decide another issue not even raised by the parties in the case. He wanted the Court on its own motion to impose sanctions against Earl Warren. He reasoned that $1,000 would be an appropriate amount. The trial court doubled his fine from

$50 to $100, and the appeals court doubled that fine. The stature of the Supreme Court, he reasoned, required that the fine now be *ten times* as much.

Wade knew that the other justices would never go along with this bizarre proposal. But the chief had worked himself into such a state that he might print the opinion anyway. Wade called Baker's chambers.

"Hi, Harry, what's the problem? Been reading about our old friend Earl Warren?"

"I'd like to come over and chat."

"By all means."

Over the years Wade had come to identify more and more with the views of Baker, except in criminal cases where he remained fiercely loyal to police agencies. He began to appreciate the role of the Court in protecting the rights of the individual and began to see through the political manipulations of the chief.

Baker was nonchalant about the Warren case when Wade arrived at his chambers. He was shocked when he read the language used by the chief but soon realized that the chief had written away any chance that the other justices would join in such an opinion. To be on the safe side, he had already dispatched his clerks to get a feel for the reaction to the opinion from the clerks in some of the other chambers. He wondered if Wade had spoken with some of the more conservative justices, the ones that would still talk to him, for their reaction.

"We have to do something," Wade said. "Have you read some of these things in here?" He was clutching the chief's opinion. He began to read before Baker could answer. "'Appellant considers the judicial system a laboratory where small boys can play. This curious sequence suggests the dangers of a system of legal education that trains students in technique without instilling a sense of professional responsibility and ethics – a bit like giving a small boy a loaded pistol without instruction as to when and how it is to be used.'"

Wade looked up, his mouth agape.

"Personally, I don't think small boys should be given loaded pistols in the first place," Baker deadpanned.

"This is no laughing matter."

"Don't worry, Harry. This won't fly and you know it, unless you have heard something I haven't. Have you?"

"So far the reaction seems to range from amusement to utter disgust. Even Usery thinks he's off his rocker."

"So what are you worried about?"

"I don't know. I just hate to see him make such a fool out of himself. It's really sad."

"He's a big boy. This is not a playground, you know. Adults only at this court."

Wade gave Baker a sidelong glance as Baker led him out with an arm around his shoulder. Baker could not bring himself to feel sorry for the chief. The chief had presided over the complete re-writing of the constitution by the court.

Many of the important gains in freedom and human dignity that Baker himself had helped to engineer years ago had been gradually eroded or cast aside altogether by the new conservative court.

Baker had found himself working harder than ever to put together coalitions of justices that would erect makeshift eddies and dams to stem the rising tide of conservatism. Increasingly he found himself with the dwindling set of like-minded justices engulfed in the torrent. They were voices in the wilderness, sounding the alarm that rights that had taken decades, not to mention bloodshed, to win were in jeopardy.

But he did manage to sabotage the onslaught somewhat, carving out safe harbors within areas like free speech or separation of church and state, where even the new radical justices would be unable to assail liberties that could now be enjoyed for generations to come.

The challenge had given Baker a new lease on life. He was energized by the task of winning these battles, even though he knew that the progressive forces had lost the war for now. He couldn't help but be pleased that he would outlast Moorehead. He had a good five years or so left in him, while Moorehead was spent and lame. Moorehead did not have the intellectual firepower to mastermind significant doctrines of law that would stand the test of time.

Moorehead did create an important legacy, however. He had managed to alter the scholarly pursuits of a major institution of the constitutional order, making the Supreme Court another of the political branches of government. In the 200 years since the Court had been established, politics always played some role among the members of the Court.

The justices were mindful of the effect of their decisions on issues of the day and the popular will of the people at any given time in history. Subconsciously at least, the justices could not help but be influenced by their personal political philosophies in their interpretation of the Constitution. But members of the Court had always tried to fashion a legal approach to their interpretations and to be faithful to the intellectual integrity of that approach.

They did not base their decisions on political theories.

During the tenure of Moorehead, a Pandora's box had been opened whereby the justices were free and, in fact, were induced to engage in political warfare with one another. The conflicting decisions of the Court could no longer be reconciled with any discernable legal doctrine. An observer could only predict the result in a given case by assessing the political nature of the dispute in question, and then count the votes of the justices based on where each stood politically on that issue.

This made politics fair game at the Court, in the press, and in the Senate when new justices were confirmed. The Court had been transformed from an apolitical institution, designed to interpret the legal meaning of the Constitution, into a political animal, the very type of institution the Court was meant to counterbalance.

Baker had become an unwitting accomplice in this gradual transformation.

In the years before Moorehead arrived, he had joined with the other members of the Court in rejecting the absolutist doctrine, which simply held that freedoms of the individual guaranteed by the Constitution could not be denied no matter what justification was offered by the political branches. The Court rejected this theory. Almost all of the justices wanted to reserve the right to decide for themselves, on a case by case approach, what the contours of the rights of the people would be in a given situation.

They did not have faith in the sweeping judgment of those who had given these rights.

Ironically, this decision created the very problem about which the chief had been screaming for the past few years. The Court, by using the case by case approach, left the lower courts and litigants guessing about the outcome in each new case, which always had a slightly different set of facts. This, in turn, led to an avalanche of litigation and appeals, as attorneys and judges tried to read the tea leaves from the growing mass of conflicting opinions issued by the Supreme Court.

Had the Court taken the simple absolutist approach, there would be little room to debate the outcome in a given case. Parties would be more certain about their rights, and less likely to take what was now a crapshoot in the courts. Judges would be less likely to guess wrong about how the votes would stack up in the Supreme Court, and fewer appeals would be filed.

The case-by-case method, together with the open political maneuvering on the Court, created the explosion of litigation about which Moorehead bitterly complained. Now he wanted to punish litigants who guessed wrong about the outcome in a case. Despite the confusion bred in the Court itself which invited litigants to take a turn with a roll of the dice, Moorehead blamed the litigants instead, mistaking disagreement with his own encrusted views with ideas truly lacking in merit.

He had now dispensed with all pretext to objectivity and tolerance toward views that differed with his own. He was rabid with hate.

At the conference the justices braced themselves for what they knew would be an unpleasant experience. When Earl's case was brought up, the chief broke with his own procedure and was the first to vote.

"The Earl Warren case. I have circulated an opinion that you have all received. I vote that the appeal be dismissed, and cert be denied. In addition, the Court must impose sanctions for this frivolous appeal, as explained in the opinion."

He looked calmly at the other justices, who sat quietly for a moment.

"Chief," Wade said softly, "I think I speak for everyone when I say that the Court cannot take such a course of action."

"You mean you speak for yourself and your friends to whom you have sold out, Harry." The rebuke came as a surprise to the justices, some of whom squirmed in their seats.

Arguments over issues often became heated, but no one ever lashed out at another justice, at least not in conference.

"If I may interject," Usery said, breaking the moment of uncomfortable silence, "There appears to be no jurisdiction of the Court over this appeal, and there seems to be no reason to grant cert, at least because of the procedural problems. None of the parties have requested sanctions. We should let the case die a natural death and move on to more important matters."

"If the case is procedurally defective, then it can be frivolous for that reason in addition to the merits," the chief retorted, failing to take the opportunity to back down. His whole prestige was on the line. He could not let Earl get away with this humiliation a second time.

"I'm not so sure the merits are all that frivolous." The comment came from Baker, who until then had been content to sit back and watch the chief self-destruct. "I agree with Justice Usery that the procedural problems prevent us from taking the case, and the record is not developed enough to make the issue suitable to hear at this time, but this young man may have a point when he argues that the imposition of sanctions by a court has a chilling effect on advocacy. Parties and attorneys may be less likely to argue novel points of law for fear that if they lose, the judge will impose sanctions. The law will suffer from the timidity to explore new avenues, new theories. If the Court were inclined to vote for sanctions on its own motion, I would have to dissent for these reasons. Particularly in this Court, we cannot punish parties for arguing new ideas with which some of us do not happen to agree."

Moorehead was shaking with rage as Baker spoke. "You want to grant cert in a, in a *traffic* case?" He was seething.

"Not at all. But neither do I want to swat a fly with a sledgehammer, Chief."

"Enough discussion," Moorehead stammered. "I have voted. We can proceed with the vote."

Each justice voted to dismiss the appeal and deny cert. None wanted to grant sanctions, and none voted to join Moorehead's opinion. As the vote progressed, the chief's face fell. The great political manipulator had failed to line up his votes before the conference and was going down to a humiliating defeat. He did not seem to care. Strangely enough, now he was standing on *his* principles. When the vote was completed, the justices looked at him expectantly.

"My decision stands," he said calmly.

"But no one voted with you, Chief," Wade said plaintively. "Then I will publish anyway."

"As what? A concurrence to denial of cert? It's never been done before. You can't," Wade said in disbelief.

"Watch me," the chief sneered, leaning forward and glaring at Wade. Then he abruptly stood and left the room. The justices all exchanged embarrassed looks.

They had not even finished voting on the cases left to decide.

CHAPTER XVI
FIFTEEN MINUTES OF FAME

Earl mounted the stairs to the bus, paid his fare, and took his usual seat in the rear next to the window. He gazed outside looking at nothing in particular. He had grown weary of taking the bus, although the long ride gave him a chance to relax and read the morning newspaper on his way to work. One way or the other, his silly traffic case would soon be resolved, and he could get his license back. Then he could join the other hapless motorists stuck in traffic.

He was thinking about Marilyn.

They had passed onto a new plateau in their relationship. The intimacy they shared had bound them together tightly. Enough time had now passed to make them both consider a long-term commitment. He knew that he was not the ideal suitor in the minds of her parents, which was not so important to him but was to her. Sitting in the back of a bus with others in the lower echelons of the economic ladder drove the point home that they were from two very different worlds.

Both of them would have to make an adjustment, and he was not sure what type of life they would share that would be fashioned from such a compromise. He wasn't sure how things would work out, but he did know that he cared very deeply for Marilyn and was certain she felt the same way about him.

Maybe that was enough.

As he walked into the office with a large coffee he had purchased on the way to work, he greeted Angie, the secretary. Angie had replaced Becky, who had replaced Marisol, who had replaced Mildred, who had, in turn, replaced Wilma – all within the past six months.

Earl started the habit of buying his coffee from the outside when Wilma confided that she put laxative in the morning coffee in her losing war against Pete, the tyrant.

Angie looked up and smiled, handing Earl his telephone messages as he passed by her desk on his way to his office. He sat down with a sigh, sorting through the pink message slips.

One was from the AP wire service. He was wondering which of his bizarre assortment of cases would prompt an AP reporter to call when he was paged by Angie.

"Earl, it's the Associated Press guy again."

"Thanks, Angie."

A reporter was on the line wanting to know his reaction to the decision of the Supreme Court announced earlier in the day.

He hesitated for a moment, trying to figure out which case he had recently taken to the Supreme Court, momentarily forgetting about his traffic case.

"What decision?"

"The decision on your traffic case."

For a split second Earl became excited. The Court had agreed to hear a traffic case, cause for some interest. At last he had broken through the barrier of stony silence and cryptic messages from the Court and would have his case heard.

"I haven't received any decision from the Court on that case. What happened?"

"Well, the Supreme Court refused to hear your case, but the chief justice wrote this incredible opinion."

His momentary feeling of excitement quickly turned into alarm, then fear. "I haven't read the opinion. What does it say?"

"Let me read it to you. Here he talks about how you argued that the fine levied against you was a violation of your right to free speech. Then he says:

'This claim, coming from an attorney, is so utterly frivolous as to not warrant any further discussion. All this suggests is that appellant considers the judicial system a laboratory where small boys can play.'

"Then later in the opinion he says, quote:

'This curious sequence suggests the dangers of a system of legal education that trains students in technique without instilling a sense of professional responsibility and ethics – a bit like giving a small boy a loaded pistol without instruction as to when and how it is to be used. Had he thus conducted himself after finishing law school and before being admitted to practice, the state would plainly have been entitled to conclude that he was unfit to be a member of the bar.'

"He concludes by saying he would impose a penalty of $1,000 against you for bringing the case. Care to comment?"

Earl was thunderstruck. His feeling of fear began to turn to panic. *My career as an attorney is over*, he thought to himself. *How can I salvage such a situation? People are going to think I am a complete crackpot.*

After a few more seconds of stunned silence, he began to regain his composure. "Did you say he would impose a $1,000 fine?"

"Right."

"Wait a second; was that a decision of the Court or just the opinion of Moorehead?"

"That was the opinion filed by Moorehead."

"Did any other justice join his opinion?"

"No."

He asked the reporter to read the Court's opinion, which simply said:

"The appeal is dismissed for want of jurisdiction. Treating the papers whereon the appeal was taken as a petition for writ of certiorari, certiorari is denied."

"You mean he wrote a *concurring* opinion to denial of cert all by himself? I've never heard of such a thing."

Earl talked at length with the AP reporter, trying to explain the reasons for what he had done. He was pleasantly surprised when he discovered that the reporter understood what he was saying and the tangled procedural mess that led to the appeal. Earl tried to give him some colorful quotes for his story. As he tried to explain his motivation for bringing the case, he realized that he didn't have a ready answer. He had difficulty finding the right words to describe his feelings of outrage and his frustration at not having the power to at least have an honest decision made on the merits of his case. He couldn't say why he did this thing. His actions sprung from deep within him as if they had a life of their own. He had had an emotional reaction without coolly calculating the risks involved – or the possible consequences of what he was doing.

Afterwards, he received a call from a reporter in Los Angeles who also wanted to discuss the case.

"What is your reaction to the language used by Moorehead referring to you as a 'small boy' playing in a laboratory and again as a 'small boy' given a loaded pistol?"

"I don't know, I guess he has some sort of fixation about little boys," Earl replied. "Have you asked him?"

"He's not talking to the press right now. I think he's catching a little heat on this he didn't expect."

Earl spent the rest of the day answering a steady stream of phone calls from newspaper reporters from across the country. A reporter from the Miami Herald came into the office with a photographer for an interview. He was interested in details about his practice and other cases he had handled. The reporter had covered a trial of two clients of Earl's who were arrested for a protest against Dr. Edward Teller, who had given a speech at the University of Miami. The reporter suspected the two were communists, a deadly sin in Miami where the Cuban exile community is known for violent reactions against anyone remotely sympathetic to commies or who are against the U.S. policy that supports right-wing death squads in Latin America.

Earl tried again to explain himself to the *Herald* reporter, who sat there regarding him with what Earl thought was a jaundiced eye.

"Earl, don't these comments of Moorehead bother you? I mean, isn't he sort of like, well, sort of like God in the legal profession?" the reporter asked.

"He's not God to me. He thinks he's God. He doesn't see the little people down here getting smashed up in the court system." The reporter remained bent, busily writing in his pad.

At the end of the interview, Earl asked how he had fared. "Very nicely."

"Did I say anything quotable?" Earl asked.

"Are you kidding? 'He's not God'? 'He thinks he's God'? 'He doesn't see the little people down here getting smashed up in the court system'? That's pretty strong stuff."

By the end of the day, Earl had talked himself silly. On the ride home on the bus, he speculated about why this story had drawn such attention from across the country. He was so busy trying to explain himself that he didn't have time to really ponder what had happened. He thought back to his radio station case and how he fell under the uncomfortable glare of publicity. He was in for another rough ride and wasn't sure what to expect.

When he got home, he called Marilyn and told her about his case and the media. "Oh my god," she said after a few moments of silence.

"You think I'm in trouble this time?"

"Earl, this is the Chief Justice of the U.S. Supreme Court. Aren't you worried about how this will affect you?"

"Right now all I'm worried about is how it will affect how you feel about me," Earl shot back. "We need to talk about some things, Marilyn. Where we stand, where we're going."

"I know. I can't talk right now, Earl," she said. "Maybe tomorrow night at the judicial reception. God, I can't believe what's going on. I hope you'll be okay."

"I'll be fine; don't worry."

Early the next morning Earl was rousted from sleep by the ring of the telephone. "You awake yet?" Marilyn asked.

"I am now," he answered, sitting up and rubbing his eyes. "So you haven't seen today's paper?"

"No. I just woke up."

"You better go read it."

"Why? What's wrong?"

"Just read it. I've got to run. See you tonight."

Earl got out of bed and went to the front door. On the floor in the hallway was the morning edition of *The Miami Herald*. He picked up the paper slowly, his eyes fixed on the front page banner headline appearing across the top of the page:

"Chief Justice Scolds Young Miami Lawyer."

In the center of the article just below the headline was a picture of Moorehead to the left, and Earl's picture to the right. Between the photos was a quote from Moorehead's opinion about him and the "God" quote he had made about the chief. Below this lead story was the apparently far less significant coverage of a mere nuclear disaster in the Soviet Union.

The long-forgotten eerie feeling he experienced in law school came over him as he read the reporter's version of the facts about which

Earl was so intimately familiar. He knew by now that news stories are hardly a complete, accurate summation of an event written without a trace of editorial license. He realized and accepted the fact that space only permits a fleeting glance at a subject that is unavoidably distorted in the process.

By a method that is alien to him and other average mortals, an event becomes "newsworthy" in the minds of journalists, and then becomes a story in which the same factors that make the event news are used as a guide to selectively report facts and print quotes that fit the "angle" of the story. This process is not necessarily bad, but most readers are not aware of the way in which the process works. Those who become the subject of a news story learn the hard way. Those who don't are less inclined to read between the printed lines appearing on the page.

The phone rang again. Jeff, who was part of the circle of friends Marilyn had joined, was on the other end. He was at the infamous party the night of his arrest. Earl was surprised to get a call from him. They were not exactly close.

"Earl, have you read that article yet?"

"Yeah. What do you think?"

"Did they quote you accurately?"

"Sure."

"Then you'd better call the reporter and tell him you didn't mean what you said."

"But I meant every word."

"But it sounds too disrespectful to Moorehead. You're going to get into a lot of trouble. Maybe you should call the reporter and ask him to print an apology."

"Don't worry, Jeff. It'll be all right. But thanks for calling."

When Earl walked into the office, Angie looked up at him with a sly grin. She was holding the phone to her ear. All of the lines were flashing.

"It's been like this all morning."

She handed him a thick stack of phone messages. The story had caused a flood of phone calls from across the country. The calls came in three groups: (1) well-wishers, (2) media, and (3) lunatics. Earl spent the day answering the phone, talking to people moved to call him long distance to congratulate him. He got calls from people who had read about his case in newspapers that he never spoke to and which had quoted him at length.

The news stories had launched a feeding frenzy by the press. This is a phenomenon known as "gang banging" in the mass media. He gave radio interviews over the phone to stations in St. Louis, Minneapolis, Los Angeles, and Atlanta, and spoke with reporters across the country. The story appeared in USA Today and *U.S. News and World Report* (next to stories about the British prime minister and the wife of the president of Russia). Earl tried to explain the important ramifications of the courts restricting access and freedom of thought, the actual issues in his appeal.

The media seemed to be more interested in the idea of a person having the temerity to appeal a traffic ticket all the way to the Supreme Court.

Earl's worries about the reaction to this story quickly eased as he spoke to more and more people. There was a vast and deep dislike of Moorehead throughout the populace. Many of the people who called said that they wished they had the chance to tell Moorehead off the way he had. They understood how he felt because many of them had also had a bad experience in court.

They derived a vicarious delight at someone appealing a traffic case to the Supreme Court.

They derided Moorehead for his arrogance and his lack of tolerance of other people's views.

Earl also answered a call and patiently listened to a woman with a complaint about her neighbors. They were Nazis, she said, who were plotting to kill her. She couldn't understand why the police would do nothing to save her. Another woman called and told Earl that the CIA had put a transmitter in her mouth. He was not sure why they decided to call him. Maybe they thought he was in a position to publicize their plight. Whatever the reason, Earl patiently listened to them and offered what little advice he could give, which usually satisfied them.

As he hung up from answering another call, Angie paged him.

"Could you come out here for a moment, Mr. Warren? There is a man here to see you."

When he came out to the reception area, he found an elderly man who had placed a large cage on Angie's desk.

Inside was his cat.

He had to bring in his cat as proof of the conspiracy against him. Someone had been sneaking into his house, night after night, slowly dying his cat red. They waited until after he was asleep because they knew he wouldn't hear them. (He wore a hearing aid and took medication that made him sleep.) As usual, the police refused to act. Earl suggested that the man set up a camera and take a picture of the culprits to catch them in the act so he could prove his case in court.

The man nodded his head in agreement.

Then he explained that he was an orphan with no family other than his cat.

"If they kill my cat, I'll kill them!" he said, his voice trembling and his eyes filling with tears.

Earl comforted him as best he could and repeated his advice. The man was grateful for the attention and decided to pay Earl for his time. He reached down and pulled off his shoe, which was soaking wet. From his shoe he pulled out a soggy $50 bill and offered it to Earl. Earl took the bill, holding it outstretched between his fingers.

Another satisfied customer, Earl thought to himself.

Other people who may otherwise be prone to surveillance by the various intelligence agencies, or extraterrestrials, are far more rational in appearance than the average person. One young man in particular came into the office. He urgently needed to speak to Earl about a case.

Earl sat down with him at some length as the man explained in detail how he had been wrongfully arrested and beaten by the police. He spoke calmly and seemed to have a good head on his shoulders. Then he said that when they asked for his fingerprints, he refused. He said that fingerprints were "property" that he owned, and he had a constitutional right to his property.

The police could not "take" his fingerprints, he said, proud of his reasoning powers.

Then he said that he was a "sovereign" and that Earl's big mistake was signing away *his* status as a sovereign when he applied for a license, which "contracted away" his rights as an individual sovereign. He had a whole book on the subject and cassette tapes distributed by a group of "sovereigns" that are still out there, lurking somewhere.

He seemed so normal at first, Earl thought to himself.

That night when Earl finally staggered into his apartment, he was physically and mentally exhausted. The publicity over the radio station case was nothing compared to this. He still had appointments next week on some radio talk shows and television stations in Miami. He wondered when the public scrutiny would die down and he could live his life in peace.

Then the phone rang. *Thank God, it's Marilyn,* Earl thought to himself. He was not up for another interview.

"How's our budding celebrity?" she asked playfully. "You wouldn't believe what I've gone through today."

"I'd believe it. The whole courthouse is talking about you and your crazy traffic case."

"I'm sorry, Marilyn. I didn't mean to embarrass you. Your friends must think I'm a real asshole."

"No, actually, they seem to think this is a screwy way to get clients. Get your name in the paper, and people will be knocking down your door to hire you."

"Yeah, right. I planned the whole thing with Moorehead in advance. He gets a percentage of my cases. All he has to do is write a blistering opinion about how rotten I am and, presto, an instant celeb."

"Are we still on for tonight?"

"If you don't mind, I'd like to stay home and nurse my wounds." The thought of attending the judicial reception, an annual gathering of hundreds of lawyers and judges, made Earl cringe. He would be the center of attention, a thought that made him shudder.

"I still want to talk to you, though."

"I have to go because of my judge, Earl. But we can get together sometime this weekend. Okay?"

"That sounds great."

The next day at the courthouse, attorneys waved and smiled at Earl. They stopped him in the hall to shake his hand and congratulate him. The substance of the story seemed to be less important than the fact that a story had been written about him. They were impressed by that fact.

Marilyn told him later that at the judicial reception the room was buzzing with talk of Earl and his case. The attorneys all thought the whole thing was funny, while some of the judges were not amused. They pumped her for information and wondered where he was.

He was glad he didn't attend. The spotlight remained on him for a few more weeks, decreasing with intensity every day. He was relieved when he could walk around again in public without the nagging suspicion that people were staring and talking about him.

During some of his interviews, he was puzzled when asked what his next step would be and how he felt about losing his case. At first he replied jokingly that he was looking into whether the World Court in The Hague could hear the case. But the questions made him realize that even though he had technically lost the appeal, he had won the case. Sort of like a Pyrrhic defeat.

He didn't understand why Moorehead wrote such an opinion, but the result was to give him much more than what he would have gotten had the Court simply denied cert. Moorehead had unintentionally called attention to Earl's case, giving him a forum to explain his ideas and concerns about the judicial system in a way that he could never have done without the chief's help.

Sure, if he had won the case in the Supreme Court, there may have been even more publicity and a new legal recourse for future litigants, but he was willing to take what Moorehead had inadvertently given him, and consider himself fortunate.

Earl had done what many lawyers spend a lifetime trying to accomplish and never do. He had attracted the attention of the Chief Justice of the United States Supreme Court, although not quite in the way other lawyers might appreciate. He had somehow gotten to Moorehead, whose ridicule and spite directed at him was regarded by Earl as a badge of honor, coming from such a despised figure in history.

He had accomplished much, Earl thought, and had a whole career ahead of him to do more.

CHAPTER XVII
WHAT GOES AROUND COMES AROUND

The chief sat in his chambers, staring absently out the window. Two weeks had passed since the Earl Warren debacle, and he was still under siege.

The clerk's office had just called again to ask him what he wanted to do with the sacks of hate mail that had accumulated in response to the Warren opinion he had written.

At least the flood of angry calls that jammed the switchboards the first two days had subsided. But the lingering effects of the case could still be felt in the hallways of the court and in public places, where he sensed the ridicule directed at him in the stares and whispers of those around him. But the views of these commoners were not of concern to him.

What had troubled him was the reaction of his colleagues and the people of substance with whom he was friendly. They all seemed to agree that this episode had placed him in a bad light and that public sentiment against him was strong. He tried to explain to them how this young rapscallion had no respect. How this kid had directly challenged him, and he had to put him in his place. But his friends told him that the public did not see things the same way, and the incident had damaged him and the Court.

Some had even suggested that maybe he was getting too old for this sort of thing. Life was too short to spend on such petty nonsense, and he wasn't getting any younger. Then last night his wife told him that she thought the strain was too much. He was starting to lose touch. She wanted him to spend the time he had left with his family. She wanted him to quit.

The accumulation of opinions from so many different people had started him to think about retirement. The reaction in this case was maybe a harbinger of future disasters. He was right to do what he did, but that was not important. The perception that he had erred so terribly that was held by so many people whose opinions mattered to him was the important consideration.

He had to consider what effect these perceptions might have on the prestige of his office and the Court, regardless of how unfair this criticism was to him. Besides which, his wife had never made such a strong appeal to him in the past on questions of his career and the Court. Maybe she was right. Maybe the time had finally come to let go.

"Rosemary," he said into the intercom, "call over to Justice Usery's chambers and see if he is available for lunch. Tell him I have an important matter to discuss."

Later that afternoon the chief would make a telephone call to the Oval Office. He wanted to give the President plenty of time to plan for the announcement he would make the following week.

As he realized the historic proportions of what he was about to do, the chief felt a curious mixture of sadness and relief.

When the announcement of the retirement of the Chief Justice of the Supreme Court was made, Earl was on his way to Marilyn's apartment for their dinner date. He was more than a little queasy about his plan to ask her about making a commitment.

He wasn't sure how he was going to approach her about the subject. When he knocked on her door, she greeted him with an excited expression.

"Guess what happened?"

"What?"

"He quit!"

"Who quit?"

"Moorehead resigned!" With that, she flung her arms around his neck and gave him a big kiss. "Can you believe it? You gave him such a hard time, the poor bastard quit. You should be ashamed of yourself for pushing around an old man like that."

Earl wasn't quite sure how to react to the news. He had more important things on his mind.

After dinner they sat on the couch, sipping what was left of the bottle of wine he had brought. He was trying to find the right opportunity to talk to her. Marilyn jumped forward and turned up the sound on the television set when she saw Moorehead being interviewed.

He said that he had retired from the bench to help work on the celebration planned for the anniversary of the Bill of Rights.

When he said that, Earl nearly choked on his wine.

Moorehead was not exactly Mr. Civil Libertarian. The reporter was also skeptical.

"You gave up one of the most powerful and important offices in government to work on *that*?" asked the incredulous reporter.

"Nothing is more important than the constitutional rights of the individual," he replied with a straight face.

Earl sat staring at the television screen, his mouth agape.

The reporter then asked him how he thought history would treat him. He said that was up to the historians. Then the reporter mentioned that he had been critical of attorneys in the past, and asked if he cared to make a comment about the attorneys that had appeared before him in more recent years. Moorehead thought for a moment. He looked very old and tired. The sagging sacs under his eyes looked almost painful. He was jowly, and his eyes were perpetually moist. He was no longer the fierce ogre that posed such a terrible threat to the civil liberties of Americans.

He was a tired, broken human being who wanted to go home.

"Well, I suppose," he said finally, "that attorneys do have a right to freedom of speech. I just wish sometimes they didn't exercise that right so often."

The screen went blank. Earl turned to Marilyn, who was still holding the remote control. "Earl, I want to talk to you about something very important," she said with a look of gravity. "I know that we are very different in a lot of ways. We come from different backgrounds, and I don't pretend to understand why you do some of the things you do. But there is one thing I *do* know." She reached out and held both of his hands, looking into his eyes with a searching expression. "I know that I love you very much, and I want to be with you always."

Earl just sat there, unable to speak.

She was the most beautiful and desirable woman in the world in that moment. "I love you, too," he whispered. They embraced in a loving, passionate kiss. "Stay with me always," she said when they pulled apart.

He held her face in his hands.

He smiled at her.
"I will, my sweet Marilyn."
"Forever."

~ FINIS ~

About the Author

James Starke is an American author and attorney who practiced law during the 1980s (and 90s). *A Matter of Principle*, his novel about the quixotic struggles of an idealistic law student, while a work of fiction, is based on actual events and experiences at a prestigious law school and in the courts.

Starke has set to work on a series of stories based on the characters developed in the novel that continue to explore true-life clashes between idealism and cynicism in the real world of law as it was practiced in the last two decades of the 20th century - an era when those who championed the cause of the less powerful found a hostile reception in the legal profession, and society in general.

This work in the sub-genre of legal fiction thus distinguishes Starke from other attorney-authors whose work is based less on literary, real-life court experiences and more so on the art of telling a story of mystery and intrigue in a courthouse setting.

www.amatterofprinciple.info

About the Cover Art

The cover art was derived from an inverted drawing by Pablo Picasso (sans squire Sancho Panza) on the front cover, that was then inverted again to face the opposite direction on the back cover:

Artist Donna Kato transformed Picasso's ink drawing into a more robust interpretation of the title character in Miguel de Cervantes' early 17th century novel The Ingenious Gentleman Don Quixote of La Mancha, from whom the main protagonist in our story apparently draws inspiration.

www.amatterofprinciple.info